Wales

by Guus Berkien

Guus Berkien has worked in Britain as a
travel guide and has written about all
areas of the country.

Above: *Nantgwynant, a beautiful valley in Snowdonia*

AA Publishing

Above: *the harp is a traditional instrument in Wales*

Front cover: *the floodlit walls of Caernarfon Castle at dusk; Cardiff's Millennium Stadium rises like a ship above the River Taff; symbols of Wales – traditional costume and daffodils*
Back cover: *Snowdon reflected in the misty waters of Llynnau Mymbyr*

Author: Guus Berkien
Translated from the Dutch by: Aletta Stevens
© 2000 Kosmos-Z&K Uitgevers B.V., Utrecht
© Maps: Bert Stamkot, Cartografisch Bureau MAP, Amsterdam
Typesetting: Studio Imago, Jacqueline Bronsema, Amersfoort
© Automobile Association Developments Limited 2001
First edition 2001. Reprinted 2004

English language edition produced for AA Publishing by: g-and-w PUBLISHING, Oxfordshire, UK
Cover design: Teo van Gerwen Design

A CIP catalogue record for this book is available from the British Library

Kosmos-Z&K publishers make every effort to ensure that their travel guides are as up to date as possible. Circumstances, however, are very changeable. Opening times and prices change, and roads are built or closed. Therefore, Kosmos-Z&K publishers do not accept liability for any incorrect or obsolete information. Assessments of attractions, hotels, restaurants and so forth are based upon the author's own experience and, therefore, descriptions given in this guide necessarily contain an element of subjective opinion which may not reflect the publisher's opinion or dictate a reader's own experience on another occasion.

We have tried to ensure accuracy in this guide, but things do change and we would be grateful for readers to advise us of any inaccuracies they may encounter.

English language edtion published by AA Publishing, a trading name of Automobile Association Developments Limited, whose registered office is Millstream, Maidenhead Road, Windsor, Berkshire, SL4 5 GD. Registered number 1878835.

A02006

Printed and bound in Italy by Printer Trento srl

Contents

About this Book

This book is divided into five sections to cover the most important aspects of your visit to Wales.

Viewing Wales pages 5–14

An introduction to Wales by the author

Features of Wales

Essence of Wales

The Shaping of Wales

Peace and Quiet

Famous of Wales

Top Ten pages 15–26

The author's choice of the Top Ten places to visit in Wales, listed in alphabetical order, each with practical information.

What to See pages 27–90

The five main areas of Wales, each with its own brief introduction and an alphabetical listing of the main attractions.

Practical information

Snippets of 'Did you know...' information

5 suggested walks

4 suggested drives

2 features

Where To... pages 91–116

Detailed listings of the best places to eat, stay, shop, take the children and be entertained.

Practical Matters pages 117–24

A highly visual section containing essential travel information.

Maps

All map references are to the individual maps found in the What to See section of this guide.

For example, the Cardiff Bay in Cardiff has the reference 🕂 73A1 – indicating the page on which the map is located and the grid square in which the museum is found. A list of the maps that have been used in this travel guide can be found in the index.

Prices

Where appropriate, an indication of the cost of an establishment is given by **£** signs:

£££ denotes higher prices, **££** denotes average prices, while **£** denotes lower charges.

Star Ratings

Most of the places described in this book have been given a separate rating:

✪✪✪ Do not miss

✪✪ Highly recommended

✪ Worth seeing

Viewing
Wales

Above: *Carreg Cennen Castle is a beautifully situated ruin in the Brecon Beacons*
Right: *the Carew Cross dates from the early 11th century*

5

Guus Berkien's Wales

Active holiday
The principality of Wales is well suited to an active holiday. Mountaineering is especially popular in Snowdonia and the Brecon Beacons, and there are many long-distance paths, both inland and along the coast. There are also opportunities for horse riding in the hills, cycling on the flat peninsulas, canoeing on the fast-flowing rivers and sailing on the lakes.

Cymru, the Celtic name for Wales, roughly translates as 'country of friends'. Visitors travelling through the principality soon discover that its inhabitants do everything to live up to this.

Welsh hospitality is one very good reason to visit the country, but there are, of course, many others – the variety of its natural beauty, for example. Firstly, the mountains with their flat tops and steep slopes, ending in deep valleys. These alternate with uplands covered in grass and heather, where sheep are the main inhabitants.

The green heart of Wales consists of rolling hills, a wide landscape intersected by narrow winding roads. The deeply indented coastline is dominated by impressive rock formations, secluded bays and deserted sandy beaches. Finally, there is a gently rolling, fertile area on the border with England, which has been most touched by human hands. Here people cluster in villages and market towns, where the influence of their English neighbours is clearly noticeable.

Wales also has fascinating reminders of an illustrious past. Welsh castles are renowned for their splendid locations, and the Edwardian castles for their solid concentric design. There are fine monastic ruins and, for those interested in industrial archaeology, there is plenty to see.

The love with which the Welsh cherish their culture and traditions undoubtedly gives the country an extra appeal. The Celtic element is found in the language, crafts and folkloric gatherings, such as eisteddfodau (► 9).

Snowdonia offers several locations that are ideal for white-water rafting

Features of Wales

Geography
Wales covers an area of 20,758sq km.
The country is divided into 22 administrative units.
The highest mountain is Snowdon (1,085m).
The maximum length (north to south) is 256km.
The maximum width (east to west) is 96km.
The coastline measures 1,232km.

The crowning ceremony is the highlight of the National Eisteddfod

People
Population – about 2.9 million, of whom 1.8 million live in the industrialised southeast.
The largest cities are the capital, Cardiff (325,000 inhabitants) and Swansea (230,000 inhabitants).
Welsh is the first language of about 20 percent of the population.

Autonomy
Wales is one of the four parts of the United Kingdom.
The principality lost its independence in 1536.
It sends 40 Members of Parliament to Westminster, including four nationalists.
A Welsh Assembly with limited powers was elected in 1999.

Welsh symbols
The principality has:
- its own flag – a red dragon on a green and white background
- its own language – Welsh
- a national anthem – *Hen wlad fy nhadau yn annwyl i mi* (The ancient land of my fathers is dear to me)
- a patron saint – St David
- a national holiday – 1 March
- its own emblems: the daffodil and the leek

Climate
Wales has a temperate sea climate. The average temperatures in the north are: 3.5°C (Jan), 8°C (Apr), 14°C (Jul) and 11°C (Oct). In the south: 4.5C° (Jan), 9°C (Apr), 16.5°C (Jul) and 11°C (Oct). The average annual rainfall is 1,350mm.

Essence of Wales

Rugby is the principality's national sport

There are more sheep than people in Wales

The Welsh emphasise and cherish the native characteristics of their country, in which their ancient Celtic culture plays an important role. You can find it in the language as well as in traditional gatherings, such as eisteddfodau, with their emphasis on the art of recital. The Welsh are very fond of theatre, poetry, debating, oratory and telling stories. They also love to sing – evident in their world-renowned male-voice choirs – while the harp features prominently in traditional Welsh music. The annual Royal Welsh Show reflects the rural nature of the principality, and the popularity of rugby as the national sport epitomises the robust sporting tastes of its inhabitants.

THE **10** ESSENTIALS

*If you only have a short time to visit Wales,
or would like to get a complete picture of
the country, here are the essentials:*

• **Climb one of Wales's famous mountains:** Snowdon (➤ 23), Cader Idris (➤ 37) or Pen y Fan.

• **Discover Welsh culture** and attend a regional or national eisteddfod or a performance of one of the many male-voice choirs.

• **Visit one of the sites of Wales's industrial past,** such as the Big Pit mine in Blaenavon (➤ 77), the Rhondda Heritage Park (➤ 82) or Llechwedd Slate Caverns in Blaenau (➤ 35).

• **Visit an Edwardian castle,** such as Caernarfon (➤ 16), Conwy (➤ 17), Harlech (➤ 38) or Beaumaris (➤ 32); view the architecturally less impressive, but splendidly located Welsh castles of Carreg Cennen (➤ 50), Castell y Bere (➤ 42) and Castell Dinas Bran (➤ 87).

• **Walk part of the Pembrokeshire Coast Path,** for example between Aberaeron and Cardigan (➤ 51), St David's and Solva (➤ 67) or Marloes and Pembroke (➤ 21, 66).

• **Visit a craft shop or woollen mill** and buy a love spoon, Celtic-style jewellery or traditional woven fabrics.

• **Buy a ticket for a rugby match,** preferably during the Six Nations Championship, and discover the enthusiasm with which the Welsh support their national sport.

• **Marvel at the extravagant interiors of Cardiff Castle** or Castell Coch (➤ 74–5), both designed by the eccentric William Burges for the third marquess of Bute.

• **Venture into one of Wales's hidden valleys,** such as the Vale of Ewyas (➤ 26), the Dysynni Valley (➤ 42), the Gwaun Valley (➤ 62) or the valley of the Senni in the Brecon Beacons (➤ 49).

• **Take a trip on one of the many tourist railways,** such as the Ffestiniog (➤ 19), Snowdon (➤ 23) or Rheidol (➤ 52).

The Pembrokeshire Coast Path winds its way along the cliffs

Eisteddfodau
Annual eisteddfodau are organised throughout the country. These traditional gatherings give ample expression to the native Celtic language and culture. Much attention is paid to poetry, literature and music (choir singing, harp and viol playing), as well as dance. A peripheral activity at these popular events is the selling of Welsh products.

The Shaping of Wales

500–100 BC
Celts occupy Wales.

c AD 78
The Romans complete the conquest of Wales.

c410
The Romans leave the province of Britannica.

c589 or 601
St David, later the patron saint of Wales, dies.

c796
Offa's Dyke built by the Mercians along the border with Wales.

844–78
Rhodri Mawr rules as king of Wales.

1039–63
Gruffydd ap Llywelyn reunites Wales.

1120
Canonisation of St David.

1188
Journey by Gerald the Welshman; his account is an important source about medieval Wales.

1195–1240
Rule of Llywelyn ap Iorwerth (the Great).

1246–82
Rule of Llywelyn ap Gruffyd (the Last).

1276–7
First Welsh War of Independence.

1282–3
Second Welsh War of Independence; death in 1282 of Llywelyn, the last independent prince.

1283
Death of Prince David, brother of Llywelyn; Edward I begins building of castles.

1284
Statute of Ruddlan: Wales is incorporated as English principality.

1301
Edward I confers the title Prince of Wales on his eldest son.

1349
Plague claims the lives of 40 percent of the population.

1485
The Welshman Henry Tudor wins the throne in the Battle of Bosworth.

1536
First Act of Union: Wales loses political and legal independence. Introduction of the county system.

1543
Second Act of Union.

1546
First printed book in Welsh.

Llywelyn ap Gruffyd was the last native prince of Wales. He died in 1282

1588
Welsh Bible translation by Bishop Morgan.

1759
Start of industrialisation in Wales.

1801
First census: 587,000 Welsh inhabitants.

1811
Welsh Methodists separate from the Church of England.

1850–60
Opening of mines in the Rhondda Valley makes Wales an important coal-producing country.

1858
First National Eisteddfod in Llangollen.

1872
Opening of University Colleges of Wales in Aberystwyth, Cardiff in 1883 and Bangor in 1884.

1876
Founding of the Football Association of Wales.

1881
Founding of the Welsh Rugby Union.

1881
Welsh Sunday Closing Act stipulates Sunday closure of pubs.

1907
Founding of National Museum (Cardiff) and National Library (Aberystwyth).

1916
David Lloyd George is the first Welsh prime minister of Britain.

1920
Founding of Anglican province: the Church in Wales.

1925
Founding of nationalist Plaid Cymru party.

c1930
The Depression leads to large-scale unemployment in the south.

1937
Regional Welsh broadcasting arm of the BBC is established.

1951
Appointment of a first minister for Wales.

1955
Cardiff becomes the official capital of the principality.

1959
Recognition of the Welsh flag.

1964
Minister for Wales promoted to Cabinet member.

1966
Election of first Plaid Cymru (National Party) Member of Parliament.

1967
Wales becomes officially bilingual.

1969
Prince Charles invested in Caernarfon as Prince of Wales.

1979
The Welsh reject the founding of a Welsh parliament in a referendum.

1982
First TV broadcasts in Welsh start on Channel 4.

1997
The Welsh vote with a tiny majority (50.3 percent) for their own assembly with limited powers.

1999
Elections for and installation of the new Welsh Assembly.

Elizabeth II invests her son Charles as Prince of Wales (1969)

Peace and Quiet

The Mynydd Preseli, part of the Pembrokeshire Coast National Park, mainly consist of upland moors

Apart from the industrialised southeast and the relatively densely populated northeast, the tranquillity and space of Wales's largely unspoiled natural beauty prevail. The rugged mountains and remote islands and peninsulas of the north, the green, partly wooded hills and valleys of the centre, and the varied coastline of the southwest are ready to be explored.

Protected areas

In order to conserve the Welsh countryside the most beautiful and valuable regions have been granted protected status. There are three national parks, spread across the country: Snowdonia, the Brecon Beacons, and the Pembrokeshire Coast.

In addition, five areas have been designated areas of outstanding natural beauty: Anglesey, the Lleyn and Gower peninsulas, the Clwydian Range, and the Wye Valley. The first three overlap with the seven coastal strips that have received the designation Heritage Coast. The others are Great Orme, Ceredigion, Pembrokeshire and Glamorgan.

As a result of their special status, these areas are well known to the public. Visitors who avoid the popular centres and leave the main routes, however, will not be bothered by crowds of other tourists.

There are also some 50 smaller nature reserves managed by regional authorities. Some of these are of great importance, such as the bird islands (limited access) of Skomer, Skokholm and Grassholm.

Forests and country parks

For economic and ecological reasons, the Forestry Commission has planted extensive coniferous forests across the principality. Recently, more attention has been paid to the leisure aspect of the forests. Visitor centres and campsites have been opened, and walking, cycling and bridle paths have been created. There has also been an attempt to make the forests more diverse with the introduction of broad-leaved trees.

In the densely populated parts of Wales, particularly in the southeastern valleys, the creation of country parks has challenged the advance of industry and house building. Although these parks can be extensive, they are sometimes slightly lacking in natural character, partly due to the provision of a wide range of facilities.

Gardens

There are not many grand gardens in the principality, but there are certainly some fine examples: Bodnant Garden in the north, Dyffryn Gardens near Cardiff (► 76), the recently reconstructed Aberglasney Gardens near Llandeilo and the new National Botanic Garden of Wales (► 20). The gardens of country houses such as Chirk Castle (► 86) and, especially, Powis Castle (► 89) are also worth a mention.

Into the mountains

The peaks of Snowdonia and the Brecon Beacons are suitable for climbing only by experienced mountaineers. Some – including Snowdon, Cader Idris and Pen y Fan – require less skill, but good physical fitness is a prerequisite.

Central Wales is less rugged and consists largely of green hills, which stretch far and wide and are sparsely inhabited. The area is suitable for exploring by car but the network of footpaths also invites devoted walkers. Touring across the twisting upland roads gives a sense of the wide, remote landscape.

Lakes (llynnoedd)

Many lakes in Wales are artificial and serve as reservoirs. They undoubtedly make a valuable contribution to the landscape, but Llyn Brianne, Llyn Vyrnwy and others cannot always hide their origins. The natural lakes, including Llyn Gwynant, Llyn y Fan Fach, Llyn y Fan Fawr, the Cregennen Lakes and Bala Lake (Llyn Tegid), are usually smaller and more in harmony with their environment. Some lakes have facilities for water sports.

The Afon Teifi at Cenarth, Ceredigion, becomes a series of rapids

Famous of Wales

Dylan Thomas
Dylan Thomas (1914–53), Wales's best-known poet and author, lived a short and turbulent life. He earned his living – with difficulty – as a writer and journalist. His most famous work, the radio play *Under Milk Wood*, was published posthumously in 1954 and was later filmed. But what stirs the imagination perhaps even more than his literary achievements was his nonconformist lifestyle. Alcohol played a major role in this and eventually led to his premature death.

Dylan Thomas used a shed as his workroom

The sons and daughters of Wales include a number of historical figures who have helped shape the history of the country.

Historic heroes
First, there is St David, the 6th-century monk and bishop, who made a significant contribution to the Christianization of Wales. St David's Day, the first of March and the feast day of this patron saint, is still celebrated – although on a limited scale.

Llywelyn ap Gruffydd (ruled 1246–82), the last native prince of Wales, is, above all, a tragic figure. With him, Wales's independence was lost forever. This is perhaps why Welsh nationalists prefer to remember Owain Glyndwr (*c*1350–1416), a heroic nobleman who dared to rebel against the English. After initial success, the rebellion was quashed due to lack of support from outside.

Politicians
20th-century politicians include David Lloyd George, the Liberal prime minister during World War I, and Aneurin Bevan, who as minister of health inaugurated the National Health Service. Neil Kinnock led the Labour Party from 1983 to 1992, before moving on to become a European Community commissioner.

Singers and pop groups

The singers Shirley Bassey and Tom Jones and the opera baritone Bryn Tyrfel are known worldwide. Popular bands include Catatonia from Cardiff and the Stereophonics from Swansea, whose albums have climbed high in the charts all over the world, as have those of the Manic Street Preachers.

Film stars
Richard Burton is well known and due to recent successes Catherine Zeta Jones and Sir Anthony Hopkins are familiar to many film-goers.

Top Ten

1
Caernarfon Castle

 28B4

✉ Castle Ditch

☎ 01286 677617

🕐 Apr–May, Oct, Mon–Sat
9:30–5, Sun 11–5;
Jun–Sep, Mon–Sat
9:30–6, Sun 11–6;
Nov–Mar, Mon–Sat
9:30–4, Sun 11–4

🚌 In the town centre

🚆 Bangor 16km (9 miles)

♿ Few

🖐 Moderate

↔ Caernarfon (➤ 35)

ℹ Castle Street
(☎ 01286 672232)

Right: *a view of the
courtyard of Caernarfon
Castle*

Previous page top: *the
Snowdon Mountain
Railway climbs to the
summit*
Previous page bottom:
*Welsh farmers stop for
a chat*

*The excellent state of preservation and its
historical associations have made this World
Heritage Site a top attraction.*

Caernarfon Castle dominates the small walled town of the
same name and the estuary of the now unimportant Afon
Seiont. The castle owes its present appearance mainly to
Edward I of England. It was founded in 1090 by the
Norman count of Chester and was rebuilt by Edward I in
1283, after the death of the last native prince. The castle's
role was not merely military: it also served as an
administrative centre and as a royal palace.
A second phase of building followed between 1296 and
1323, paying particular attention to the town side of the
castle.

Since the Welsh in the north were kept under control
partly from here, Caernarfon Castle was for many the
symbol of English supremacy. The first English prince of
Wales was born within the castle walls in 1284 and was
invested in 1301; the investiture of Edward VIII took place
in 1911, and that of the current prince of Wales, Charles,
on 1 July 1969.

The walls and towers, which offer fantastic views,
are all accessible after the 19th- and 20th-century
restorations; the original residential quarters have survived
less well.

2
Conwy

This medieval town, a UNESCO World Heritage Site, also has an impressive castle.

The late 13th-century walls that enclose the old town of Conwy include 22 towers and three gateways. They protect a maze of small streets, lined by a variety of historic buildings.

Predominant is the 14th-century St Mary's Church, incorporating a remnant of a 12th-century Cistercian abbey. Then there is the restored **Aberconwy House**, a 14th-century timber-framed merchant's dwelling. It has an authentic interior and now serves as a museum. Likewise **Plas Mawr**, an Elizabethan mansion built between 1576 and 1585 for the influential merchant Robert Wynn. The Smallest House by contrast, a fisherman's cottage on the quayside, measuring 1.8m by 3m by 2.5m, claims to be the smallest house in Britain.

Conwy Castle enforces the historic nature of the town and its eight massive towers are visible all around. The fortress was once part of the iron ring of Edwardian castles, but – unlike its contemporaries – is not concentric in plan. The natural defences of the site made it unnecessary to have extra walls.

Two of the three bridges that cross the River Conwy deserve special attention: Telford's 327m-long suspension bridge dating from 1826, and Stephenson's railway bridge from 1848. In addition, Conwy (1,400 inhabitants) has a teapot museum and a butterfly garden.

Telford's suspension bridge (1826) and Conwy Castle

✚ 29C5

Conwy Castle

☎ 01492 592358

🕐 Apr–May, Oct, Mon–Sat 9:30–5, Sun 11–5; Jun–Sep, Mon–Sat 9:30–6, Sun 11–6; Nov–Mar, Mon–Sat 9:30–4, Sun 11–4. Closed Christmas, New Year

🚌 5 from Llandudno and Bangor

🚆 Conwy (Chester–Holyhead line)

♿ Few

✋ Moderate

ℹ️ Conwy Castle Visitor Centre (☎ 01492 592248)

Aberconwy House

🕐 Apr–Oct, Wed–Mon 11–5

♿ Few

✋ Cheap

Plas Mawr

🕐 Apr–Jun, Sep, Tue–Sun 9:30–5; Jun–Aug, Tue–Sun 9:30–6; Oct, Tue–Sun 9:30–4

♿ Few

✋ Moderate

3
Cregennen Lakes

The isolated Cregennen Lakes near Dolgellau

Two small mountain lakes, idyllically situated between the foothills of Cader Idris.

28B4 (not marked on map – just west of Cader Idris)

28 Dolgellau–Tywyn stops in Arthog, 2km (1½ miles) northwest

Morfa Mawddach (Barmouth–Tywyn line) is 3km (2 miles) from Arthog

Free

Cader Idris (► 37)

The Cregennen Lakes (Llynnau Cregennen) are situated at an altitude of 300m in the western shadow of Cader Idris. The open character of the surrounding area provides an uninterrupted view of the north face of the mountain range and of the nearby coastline. The area is the property of the National Trust, which received it as a gift from Major Wynne-Jones in memory of his two sons, who both perished in World War II.

There are two ways to reach the area by car. The simplest route is the unnumbered road from Dolgellau which at the start runs beside the Ty Nant car park and the Gwernan Lake Hotel, from where two paths lead to the summit of Cader Idris (892m).

The alternative route, which winds its way up from Arthog, is perhaps less suitable for cars, as the road is narrow, steep and winding. Moreover, there will be several gates to open and close. It is less awkward on foot and you will then have time to enjoy the magnificent panorama across Barmouth and the Mawddach estuary.

There is a car park beside the larger lake, which can be used as a starting point for walks or picnics. The remote location of this beauty spot ensures that the area is seldom crowded.

4
Ffestiniog Railway

A trip on the steam train along the 22km narrow-gauge track of the Ffestiniog Railway is one of the top attractions in north Wales.

The railway was built in the 1830s as a horse-drawn tram to transport slate from the quarries of Blaenau Ffestiniog to Porthmadog harbour. The horses were withdrawn in 1863 and replaced by specially designed steam trains, and a year later permission was granted to carry passengers.

By 1946 the demand for slate had decreased considerably, which led to the abrupt closure of the by then uneconomic line. Several years later, railway enthusiasts breathed new life into the Ffestiniog Railway and in 1955 it was partly reopened. On 25 May 1982 the entire track was passable again.

Trips start at Porthmadog harbour and lead across a dam built in 1811 (the Cob) towards Minffordd. The route then passes the slopes above the green, densely wooded Vale of Ffestiniog to go up towards the barren landscape of the Tanygrisiau Reservoir. The journey ends in the sombre slate town of Blaenau Ffestiniog.

The trip takes one hour. It is possible to break the journey at Tan-y-Bwlch, Plas Halt or Dduallt for a walk in the surrounding forests.

28B4

Harbour Station, Porthmadog

01766 512340

Apr–Oct, the first train leaves Porthmadog at 10:25; Nov–Mar, limited service at weekends and holiday periods

Buffet in most trains; café/restaurant in Porthmadog Harbour Station; pub in Porthmadog; simple café at Tan-y-Bwlch (May–Sep)

Both Porthmadog and Blaenau are easy to reach by bus

Porthmadog and Minffordd (link with Pwllheli and Barmouth), and in Blaenau (link with Conwy and Betws-y-coed)

Good in certain trains. Special facilities at Porthmadog and Blaenau stations

Moderate; discount for children

Llechwedd Slate Caverns in Blaenau (► 35)

Porthmadog, Station Yard (☎ 01766 512981); Blaenau, High Street (only in peak season, ☎ 01766 830360)

5
National Botanic Garden of Wales

28B2

Middleton Hall Estate, Llanarthne. Take the B4310 off the A48 or A40

01558 668768

Daily 10–4:30, 5 or 6, depending on the season. Last admission one hour before closing

Café/restaurant on-site; pubs in Llanarthne and Llanddarog

279 from Carmarthen (limited service)

Camarthen and Llandeilo

Very good

Moderate

Carmarthen, Lammas Street (☎ 01267 231557); Llandeilo, car park, Crescent Road (☎ 01558 824226)

Above: the massive span of the Great Glasshouse, wth Paxton's Tower in the distance

This attraction opened in May 2000 and is the first new botanic garden to be created in the United Kingdom for two centuries.

The Middleton Hall Estate in the rural Tywi Valley (Carmarthenshire) was selected as the location for one of the most prestigious millennium projects in Britain: the £43.4 million National Botanic Garden of Wales.

In the centre of this complex stands the futuristic Great Glasshouse measuring 100m by 60m, the largest glasshouse under a single roof in the world, whose glass panels cover 4,500sq m. The interior features the endangered environments of Mediterranean Europe, South Africa, southwestern Australia, Chile and California. A sandstone ravine, rock formations and waterfalls have been built for this purpose.

The eye-catching parts of the other more formal gardens (which together account for approximately one-third of the Garden) include, first of all, the 220m Broad Walk, a herb-lined path enlivened by fountains and a whimsical stream. The concentric Double Walled Garden is also worth seeing. This is a renovated part of the late-18th-century estate created here in 1785 by the first owner, the powerful and rich banker Sir William Paxton. Other original estate features include the seven lakes, a number of waterfalls and many other structures, including the curious Paxton's Tower (1811) on a hill further away. Middleton Hall itself burned down in 1931.

6

Pembrokeshire Coast Path

A magnificent 299km (186-mile) long-distance path, which follows the splendid Pembrokeshire coastline.

Broad Haven is one of many picturesque bays along the Pembrokeshire coastline

Rugged cliffs, deep ravines, wide bays, deserted sandy beaches and, above all, bizarre rock formations: all await the walker who follows (even part of) the Pembrokeshire Coast Path. This is undoubtedly one of the most attractive of the 13 National Trails of Great Britain, because of the varied landscape and characteristic fishing villages along the way, as well as the fascinating flora and wildlife. The path forms part of the national park of the same name.

Only visitors with ample time will be able to complete the entire route and this would take at least two weeks. Most walkers limit themselves to shorter distances. Several sections are suitable for a day trip:

- From Abereiddy (Blue Lagoon) to the harbour of Porthgain.
- From St Justinian via Porthclais to Caerfai Bay (near St David's).
- Either side of the fishing village of Solva, a small resort nestling in a deep inlet.
- From Martin's Haven via Gateholm Island to Marloes Sands.
- From St Govan's Head westward via St Govan's Chapel to the Elegug Stacks and the Green Bridge of Wales (rock formations in sea), or eastward via Broad Haven to Barafundle Bay and Stackpole Quay.
- From Manorbier Bay via Skrinkle Haven and Lydstep Point to Lydstep Haven.

The Pembrokeshire Coast National Park information centres have a range of maps for sale, which describe sections of the Pembrokeshire Coast Path. There are also brochures available in the extensive National Park Walk Series, which are very useful.

➕ 28A1–A2

🚌 Possible starting or finishing points accessible by bus: St David's (411), Solva (411), Bosherston (395), Manorbier (349) and Lydstep (349). For frequency and times
☎ 01437 775227

ℹ️ National park information centres in St David's (☎ 01437 720392) and Newport (☎ 01239 820912). Tourist information centres in Tenby, The Crort (☎ 01834 842404); Pembroke, Commons Road (☎ 01646 622388); Haverfordwest, Old Bridge (☎ 01437 763110)

7
St David's Cathedral

The nave of St David's Cathedral

For both its location and architecture, this is the finest cathedral in Wales.

+ 28A2

✉ Centre of St David's

☎ 01437 720202

🕐 Daily 8–7

🚌 411 from Haverfordwest and Fishguard

🚉 Haverfordwest and Fishguard

♿ Good

💷 Free, contribution

↔ St David's (➤ 67); Pembrokeshire Coast Path (➤ 21)

ℹ The Grove (☎ 01437 720392)

❓ The annual St David's Cathedral Music Festival in May–Jun (☎ 01437 720271)

Nothing remains of the monastery built by St David in the Alun Valley around the year 550. The present cathedral dates from later in the Middle Ages and bears the features of many different styles. The arcades of the 12th-century nave are clearly Romanesque, but the rich decoration points to a transition to the Gothic style. The side windows and triforium date from the time of Bishop Henry Gower (1328–47), who had almost the entire building changed into the Decorated style. The elaborately carved stone partition between the nave and the choir (with Gower's tomb) is 14th century, whereas the fine wooden ceiling, the 28 choir stalls, the bishop's seat and other striking woodcarvings are late 15th century.

Of special interest also are the vaults of the crossing and choir, the shrine (destroyed during the Reformation) and relics of St David, to the side of the choir and behind the main altar respectively, and the many chapels and graves of bishops and noblemen, including the tomb in the choir of Henry VII's father, Edmund Tudor, dating from 1456.

The 13th-century Porth y Twr, the only remaining entrance gate to the cathedral close, offers a fine view across the valley. The cathedral is built from a local stone that has a purplish glow.

The Bishop's Palace adjacent to the church is an atmospheric ruin from the mid-14th century.

8
Snowdon

*Wales's highest mountain (1,085m) is
climbed by thousands of people every year.*

The 8km Llanberis Path is the longest but also the easiest
route to the summit. It is used by some 1,500 climbers a
day. The ascent takes about three hours, the descent
slightly less. The Halfway Café provides a rest.

Three beautiful routes start at the Pen-y-Pass car park, on
the south side of the Pass of Llanberis. As this car park fills
up early in the day, it is better to use the Sherpa bus services
(95) from Llanberis or Nant Peris (Park & Ride).

The Miners' Track (6.5km, 2½ hours one way), which
runs along the deserted lakes of Llyn Llydaw and Llyn
Glaslyn, is relatively easy. This also applies to the somewhat
steeper, slightly more northern Pyg Track (5.5km, 2½ hours
one way). The Grib Goch Route is only suitable for
experienced climbers.

Two sections start on the Caernarfon–Beddgelert road
(A4085). Both are manageable and, for that reason, very
popular. The Snowdon Ranger Path (6.5km) starts at the
youth hostel on the shores of Llyn Cwellyn, and the Pitt's
Head Track (6.5km) at the National Trust car park, just south
of Rhyd-Ddu.

The Watkin Path (6.5km, 3 hours one way) is not easy
and starts at Bethania Bridge, 5km (3 miles) north of
Beddgelert (A498).

The Sherpa bus service makes it possible to return by a
different path from the one used to go up. It is, of course,
also possible to take the **Snowdon Mountain Railway** for
the journey there or back. This mountain railway track
opened in 1896 and covers the 7.5km route in one hour.
Return ticket holders have priority, so it is advisable in the
summer season to arrive early.

✛ 28B4

Snowdon Mountain Railway

✉ In the centre of
Llanberis

☎ 01286 870223

🕐 Mid-Mar to Oct,
Sun–Fri 9–5, Sat 9–3:30

🍴 Simple restaurant on
summit

🚌 77 and 86 from Bangor;
88 from Caernarfon; 95
(Sherpa bus) from
Caernarfon and
Beddgelert, in summer
only

♿ Wheelchair transport
possible. Phone in
advance

✋ Fairly expensive

ℹ 41a High Street
(summer only,
☎ 01286 870765)

*A breathtaking view from
the summit of Snowdon*

9

Tintern Abbey
and the Wye Valley

These inspiring monastic ruins in the wooded Wye Valley, an Area of Outstanding Natural Beauty, are among the most beautiful in Britain

Tintern Abbey was founded in 1131 for the Cistercian order, and was rebuilt and extended between 1269 and 1301 under the patronage of Roger Bigod, lord of nearby Chepstow. In 1536 the monastery was closed by Henry VIII, and soon afterwards was robbed of its roof and given over to the elements.

The Cistercians with their sober lifestyle and their characteristic white, woollen habits, had a preference for isolated areas, which they then cultivated. In the Middle Ages, the Wye Valley was such a place. Nowadays, partly because of tourism, this is no longer so, but the location retains its rural character.

The ruined monastery is also interesting for its architecture. The roofless skeleton clearly shows the features of the Gothic Decorated style. It is no surprise, therefore, that Tintern Abbey was visited by tourists as early as the 18th century, its popularity stimulated by the poetry of William Wordsworth and by the brush of the painter

29D1

Tintern Abbey

✉ Tintern, 10km (6 miles) north of Chepstow

☎ 01291 689251

🕐 Apr–May, Oct, daily 9:30–5; Jun–Sep, daily 9:30–6; Nov–Mar, Mon–Sat 9:30–4, Sun 11–4. Closed Christmas and New Year

🚌 69 Chepstow–Monmouth

🚉 Chepstow

♿ Good

✋ Cheap

ℹ Chepstow, Bridge Street (☎ 01291 623772); Monmouth, Shire Hall (☎ 01600 713899)

❓ For special events, such as singing and theatre, please enquire on site or at the tourist information centres

The romantic ruins of Tintern Abbey lie hidden in the Wye Valley

J.M.W. Turner. It was especially the evocative and picturesque nature of the ruins that attracted these two romantic artists.

The most attractive part of the Wye Valley is the 26km (16-mile) section between Chepstow and Monmouth, and which includes Tintern. The best way to explore the valley on foot – which is certainly recommended – is to use the most southern part of Offa's Dyke Path on the English side of the river or the Wye Valley Walk (▶ 90).

Chepstow (Casgwent) is a pleasant historic market town with an impressive castle built between the 11th and 14th centuries. **Chepstow Castle** is strategically placed above the river, close to the spot where it flows into the Severn. An entrance gateway and a length of the medieval town defences, the Port Wall, also survive.

The earlier importance of Monmouth (Trefynwy), including its role as county town, is reflected in its elegant historic buildings, such as the Shire Hall, which together with some time-honoured inns surround the central Agincourt Square. A statue of Charles Steward Rolls is a tribute to the co-founder of Rolls-Royce, which originated in this area. There is also a statue of Henry V. Little remains of the castle where Henry was born in 1397, but there is a unique building that has fortunately survived from the Middle Ages: the Monnow Bridge, with a 13th-century fortified gateway protecting the town.

There are several museums in Monmouth. These feature the regional regiment, the history of the town and surroundings, and Admiral Nelson, the hero of the Battle of Trafalgar.

The medieval gateway on the Monnow Bridge in Monmouth

Chepstow Castle

✉ Bridge Street

☎ 01291 624065

🕐 Apr–May, Oct, daily 9:30–5; Jun–Sep, daily 9:30–6; Nov–Mar, Mon–Sat 9:30–4, Sun 11–4. Closed Christmas and New Year

🚆 Chepstow

✋ Cheap

ℹ Castle car park, Bridge Street (☎ 01291 623772)

10
Vale of Ewyas

A small, isolated valley in the Black Mountains, the eastern part of the Brecon Beacons National Park.

The Vale of Ewyas is perfect for walkers

Hidden among the green slopes between Llanvihangel Crucorney and Hay-on-Wye is a breathtaking area of natural beauty. The Vale of Ewyas, following the Honddu river, is an excellent area for walking and riding, but motorists following the minor road along the river will also enjoy it, provided you take care to avoid particularly busy times. The single-track road with hedgerows on either side is best avoided at weekends and on bank holidays.

The 29km (18-mile) section starts at the village of Llanfivangel Crucorney, where the Skirrid Inn claims to be one of the oldest in Wales. The road winds its way northwards through a densely wooded part of the valley, and soon follows the turning to Cwmyoy, a remote hamlet on the opposite slope. The 13th-century church, leaning from subsidence, is certainly worth a visit, but the lane leading to it is very narrow and there is barely room to park, so it is best to go on foot.

The second stopping place along the valley is an absolute must. **Llanthony Priory**, founded in 1118 and dissolved in 1538, is one of the most beautifully situated monastic ruins in Britain. The early Gothic church has pointed nave arcades dating from 1180–1230, which form an elegant contrast against the green valley. The former Prior's House is now fitted out as an inn (▶ 104).

Past Capel-y-ffin, with its small white church (1762), the road steeply climbs out of the valley towards open land and finally reaches the 542m Gospellpas, guarded by the 676m Hay Bluff from which there are wonderful views.

Then begins the descent, with splendid views towards Hay-on-Wye (Y Gelli), the friendly market town famous for its many second-hand bookshops and its annual Festival of Literature held in May.

 29C/D2

Llanthony Priory

Abbey Hotel (hotel with restaurant)

20 from Llanvihangel Crucorney and 39 from Hay-on-Wye

Abergavenny (17km/10 miles)

Good

 Free

Hay-on-Wye, Oxford Road (☎ 01497 820144); Abergavenny, Monmouth Road (☎ 01873 857588)

What to See

Above: *water-sports enthusiasts on the north beach of Llandudno*
Right: *a Welsh hill farmer*

WALES

0   20   40 km
0   10   20   30 m

Amlwich

Holyhead

Llanerchymedd   Beaumaris

Isle of
Anglesey

Holy I   Llanfair-PG   Bango

Menai St

Caernarfon

Caernarfon   Llanberis
Bay   1085m

Snowdon Bl.
Beddgelert   Ffes

Ffestiniog Railway

Nefyn   Porthmadog

Pwllheli   Portn

Llyn

Aberdaron   **Harlech Castle**   Snowd

Cregennen Lakes   Dolg

Barmouth

Cade

Cardigan

Bay   Tywyn

Irish Sea

Aberystwyth

Abaraeron

Cardigan   Lampeter

Pembrokeshire Coast
National Park

Fishguard

Gwaun   **Mynydd**
Valley   **Preseli**

St David's

Carmarthen   Llandeilo
St Clears

**National Botanic
Gardens of Wales**   C

Skomer

Milford Haven   Carew   Laugharne

Kidwelly

Saundersfoot   Llanelli

Skokholm

Pembroke   Tenby

Manorbier   *Carmarthen*
Bay   **Swansea**

Pembrokeshire
Coast National Park   Rhossili   **Gower**

Bris

A   B

dudno
Rhyl
Colwyn Bay
Denbigh
anrwst
Ruthin
etws-y-Coed
Corwen
Llangollen
Bala
Chirk Castle
t. Park
Oswestry
as-
dwy
Llanfyllin
ynlleth
Welshpool
Severn
ENGLAND
Llanidloes
Llangurig
Ludlow
il's Bridge
Rhayader
Elan Valley
Knighton
Llandrindod Wells
Builth Wells
Leominster
_yn_
nne
Llanwrtyd Wells
Hay-on-Wye
Wye
ndovery
Talgarth
Hereford
Brecon
Vale of Ewyas
Crickhowell
Three Castles
Ross-on-Wye
Gloucester
M50
recon Beacons National Park
Abergavenny
Monmouth
Blaenafon
Tredegar
Raglan Castle
Wye Valley
The Valleys
Tintern Abbey
Merthyr Tydfil
Chepstow
M48
M5
t
ot
Rhondda
Caerphilly Castle
Caerleon
Pontypridd
Castle Coch
M4
Bridgend
Llandaff Cathedral
Newport
M4
cawl
CARDIFF
Avonmouth
M4
Dyffryn Gardens
M5
hannel
C
Cardiff
Weston
Bristol
D

Birkenhead
Liverpool
M62
M5
M56
M53
Flint
Mersey
M56
Gwydian Range
Chester
M5
Wrexham
Dee
Shrewsbury
Telford
M54

Northwest Wales

Northwest Wales is taken up almost entirely by the Snowdonia National Park and by two isolated areas of outstanding natural beauty: the low island of Anglesey and the undulant Lleyn Peninsula.

All these areas feature the natural beauty of rugged mountains and valleys, dense forests and barren plateaus, rocky coastlines and wide estuaries. Sturdy castles, country mansions with fine interiors, spectacular narrow-gauge railways, mines and craft shops provide the necessary variety. But above all, northwest Wales is the domain of the active visitor: the mountaineer, walker, horse rider, angler and water-sports enthusiast.

'Ever charming, ever new,
When will the landscape tire the view!
The fountain's fall, the river's flow,
The woody valleys, warm and low;
The windy summit, wild and high,
Roughly rushing on the sky!'

JOHN DYER
(1699–1757) *Grongar Hill*

———————————•———————————

Left: *the Swallow Falls at Betws-y-coed*

Opposite: *Beaumaris Castle is one of the main sights on Anglesey*

 28B5

Beaumaris Castle
- ✉ Town centre
- ☎ 01248 810361
- 🕐 Apr–May, Oct: daily 9:30–5; Jun–Sep, daily 9:30–6; Nov–Mar, Mon–Sat 9:30–4, Sun 11–4. Closed Christmas and New Year
- 🚌 53 and 57 from Bangor
- 💷 Cheap
- ❓ For events (theatre), enquire on site

Plas Newydd
- ✉ 3.5km (2 miles) southwest of Llanfair PG on the A4080 to Brynsiencyn
- ☎ 01248 714795
- 🕐 Apr–Oct, Sat–Wed 12–5, garden 11–5:30
- 🚌 42 from Bangor
- ♿ Good
- 💷 Moderate
- ❓ For events, enquire on site

ANGLESEY (YNYS MÔN) ⊙⊙

The island's secluded location beyond the Menai Strait so beloved by water-sports enthusiasts has helped to preserve its traditional rural and Celtic character. This is one of the regions where the majority of inhabitants speak Welsh and where everything is on a small scale.

Many of Anglesey's visitors rightly focus on the 200km (125 miles) coastline. In addition to secluded, rocky coves and inlets, such as Porth Eilian, Porth Wen, Porth Dafarch and Porth Swtan (Church Bay), there are numerous long and narrow bays with clean sandy beaches, where sunbathers and swimmers flock – Benllech, Red Wharf Bay, Trearddur Bay, Llanddwyn. There are also other strips of coastline that are popular with surfers and water-sports enthusiasts: Bull Bay, Porth Tywyn-mawr, Traeth Llydan (Silver Bay) and, above all, Rhosneigr.

Special sights include the moated late 13th-century **Beaumaris Castle**, the Museum of Childhood, the 17th-century Courthouse, the Victorian prison and the medieval inns in Beaumaris (Biwmares). There is also **Plas Newydd**, the 18th-century residence of the marquess of Anglesey, which is worth visiting both for its interior and its gardens. The nearby Marquis of Anglesey's Column (115 steps) offers a magnificent view, including Telford's 386m-long Menai Suspension Bridge (1826), the first iron suspension bridge in the world, and Stephenson's 450m Britannia Bridge (1850), which is used by vehicles and trains. Llanfairpwllgwyngyllgogerychwyrndrobwllllandysiliogogogoch is internationally renowned for having the longest place name in the world.

Nature lovers can walk amid the pines of Newborough Forest (800ha), which borders the national nature reserve of Newborough Warren, with its long stretches of dunes and fascinating wildlife. Near the 220m Holyhead Mountain on Holy Island stands the Ellen's Tower Seabird Centre.

DID YOU KNOW?

It is said that the place name Beddgelert means 'Gelert's grave'. This is supposed to refer to Prince Llywelyn's dog, who was left to guard his son. When the Prince returned to find his son covered in blood, he thought the dog was responsible and he beat the animal to death. Later he discovered that Gelert had saved his son from the clutches of a wolf.

BEDDGELERT

This is a picturesque mountain village with cottages built of stone set around a remarkable bridge, split in two by the fast-flowing Glaslyn river and enclosed by steep slopes. There are a number of pleasant establishments for food and drink, or spending the night, but it is the surrounding area which demands special attention.

Nantgwynant is one of the most attractive valleys in Snowdonia, especially where the road passes Llyn Dinas and Llyn Gwynant. Follow the A498 until a kilometre before the Llanberis turning for a breathtaking panorama. There is ample parking on the left. The **Sygun Copper Mine** is another attraction in this valley. It is situated less than 2km (1½ miles) outside the village.

South of Beddgelert is the beautiful Pass of Aberglaslyn, which can be traversed along the now deserted section of the Welsh Highland Railway.

🞤 28B4

Sygun Copper Mine
✉ A498, 2 km (1½ miles) northwest of Beddgelert
☎ 01766 510100/510101
🕐 Feb–Nov, daily 10–5
🚌 95 from Beddgelert
♿ Moderate

Below: *Sygun Copper Mine in the Gwynant valley*

28B5

BETHESDA ⊕⊕

A mining village may not seem a very cheerful place, but this one is certainly characteristic of the region, surrounded by plentiful evidence of former slate quarries. The nearby Nant Ffrancon Pass leads up towards Llyn Ogwen in the very heart of Snowdonia. From there it is possible to look across the entire length of the valley, but the neighbouring peaks of the Carneddau (maximum 1044m) and the Glyders (maximum 994m) are equally impressive. The Ogwen Falls just below Llyn Ogwen are just one of the many beauty spots in this area. Two others are the nature reserve of Cwm Idwal with the mountain lake of Llyn Idwal, and the rocks of Twll Du (Devil's Kitchen) that tower above it.

29C4
✉ Royal Oak Stables
☎ 01690 710426
🚉 Betws-y-coed

BETWS-Y-COED ⊕⊕

Betws-y-coed, which is easily accessible by train, has been known since Victorian times for its fine countryside. It has grown into a popular stopping place with many tourist facilities. In addition to the hotels, places to eat and drink, and souvenir shops, there are a number of small museums for railway and car enthusiasts. There is also an excellent national park visitor centre in the village.

Next to Telford's iron Waterloo Bridge (1815) stands the eye-catching, centrally positioned Pont-y-Pair bridge. This is a good starting point for walks in the immediate vicinity. Those looking for a nearby goal can visit the Swallow Falls beyond the Miners' Bridge, 5km (3 miles) west on the A5; or the Fairy Glen and Conwy Falls, 3.5km (2 miles) east on the A5.

Penmachno, on the B4406 south of Conwy Falls, with a woollen mill of the same name (guided tours), is a little further and therefore best reached by car. The same applies to the extensive Gwydir Forest, with its numerous trails, including those to the remote lakes of Llyn Crafnant Reservoir and Llyn Geirionydd, as well as to Dolwyddelan Castle, a 13th-century square tower – once the court of Llywelyn ap Iorwerth (the Great), now a solitary structure in the sweeping landscape.

Nant Ffrancon is a characteristic Snowdonian valley

BLAENAU FFESTINIOG ✪

This terminus of the fascinating Ffestiniog Railway (➤ 19) owes its rise and fall to the exploitation of slate. The town once had 12,000 inhabitants, now there are less than half that number. Blaenau, which is surrounded by desolate mountain tops, has the sombre grey – and in rain even inhospitable – appearance of a typical mining village. The main attraction is the **Llechwedd Slate Caverns**, of which the most interesting parts are the Miners' Tramway Tour through tunnels and caves, and the Deep Mine Tour, which takes visitors down into the depths on special trains.

 28B4

Llechwedd Slate Caverns
☎ 01766 830306
🕐 Mar–Sep, daily 10–5:15; Oct–Mar, 10–4:15. Closed Christmas and New Year
🍴 Yes
🚉 Blaenau Ffestiniog
♿ Moderate. Visitors with disabilities who have folding wheelchairs can take part in the Deep Mine Tour
💷 Fairly expensive
ℹ Blaenau, High Street (☎ 01766 830360)

Llechwedd Slate Caverns

CAERNARFON ✪✪✪

Most visitors are drawn by the impressive castle (➤ 16), but the town itself is also worthy of attention. The old quarter is still surrounded by late 13th-century walls built with the castle, and the 14th-century St Mary's Church is incorporated in these defences. Close to the church (Victoria Dock) is a maritime museum.

The remains of **Segontium**, a Roman fort built in AD 78 on a site higher up, may not be spectacular but they are interesting to enthusiasts. It is said that the Emperor Constantine the Great was born here in 280. The excavations also include a small museum.

Dinas Dinnle, 8km (5 miles) southwest, has a good beach as well as an airfield that offers flights around the area.

✚ 28B4

Segontium
✉ Beddgelert Road, southeast of the centre
☎ 01286 675625
🕐 Apr–Oct, Mon–Sat 10–5, Sun 14–5; Nov–Mar, Mon–Sat 10–4, Sun 14–4
♿ Good
💷 Cheap

CONWY (➤ 17, TOP TEN)

35

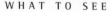

+ 28B4
i Eldon Square
☎ 01341 422888

*The town of Dolgellau is
an ideal touring base*

CREGENNEN LAKES (► 18, TOP TEN)

DOLGELLAU ●●

As is often the case in Wales, the town derives its charm
and touristic importance from the splendid mountain
landscape around it. The town itself looks rather sombre: it
is almost entirely built of slate. The centre is threaded by
narrow alleyways, some of which lead into the central Eldon
Square. There is a small museum devoted to the Quaker
movement, which had its origins here. At the Gwynfynydd
Gold Centre in Lion Yard it is possible to book a visit to the
Gwynfynydd mine in the Coed-y-Brenin Forest, where they
still dig for gold (daily in summer, not on Sundays in winter).

The area around Dolgellau is excellent walking country.
The Cregennen Lakes (► 18) and the routes to the top of
Cader Idris (► 37) are described elsewhere.

The Torrent Walk of some 3km (2 miles) starts at
Caerynwch, east of the town, and follows the wooded
Clywedog valley. The Precipice Walk (starting near Nannau,
on the road to Llanfechreth) is 5.5km (3.5 miles) and runs
along Llyn Cynwch before climbing to heights that offer a
splendid view across the Mawddach estuary and the Cader
Idris range.

Finally, the Maddach Walk of 26km (16 miles) there and
back (starting at the A470/A493 junction) leads to the
estuary of the river of the same name. Route descriptions
are available at the tourist information centre in Eldon
Square.

The best place to obtain information about walking and
cycling in the huge Coed-y-Brenin Forest is the Forestry
Commission's Maesgwm Visitor Centre on the A470 north
(Ganllwyd).

To the Top of Cader Idris

The first two routes start from the minor road leading from Dolgellau past Llyn Gwernan to the Cregennan Lakes. For the Pony Path you can start at the Ty–nant Farm car park, 4km (2.5 miles) outside Dolgellau.

This is a 10km (6-mile) trip there and back, and takes four to five hours. The last part is fairly steep, but the section as a whole is quite manageable.

The trip along the Foxes' Path starts at Gwernan Lake Hotel, 2.5km (1.5 miles) outside Dolgellau.

It is possible to cover some 7km (4 miles) in about five hours. The path has been badly affected by erosion, so it is fairly rocky and difficult to negotiate. The use of this section is not recommended for inexperienced walkers.

For the third route you will need to skirt partly round the Cader Idris range from Dolgellau towards the junction of the A487 and the B4405. This route follows the Minffordd Path. Your starting point is the Minffordd car park.

This route is 9.5km (6 miles) long and takes about five hours. It is the shortest, but also the steepest and most dramatic section. The steady climb goes past waterfalls and through a nature reserve, including the mountain lake of Llyn Cau.

The 'Seat of Idris', named after a mythical warrior, giant or poet, is an elongated mountain range with five peaks, which thousands of visitors climb every year. The highest peak (from where you can see Ireland on a clear day) is the 893m Penygadair.

A fourth route starts in Llanfihangel-y-pennant, at the end of the isolated Vale of Dysynni: the total distance is 16km (10 miles); duration approximately 7 hours.

Whichever of the four routes you take, according to legend it is advisable to be back before dark, since whoever spends the night on the mountain will wake up the next morning either mad, blind or as a poet. At the least, you should take adequate refreshments for the walks.

Information
Descriptive brochures of all routes are available from the national park offices. For the weather forecast, phone Mountain Call on 0891 500449.

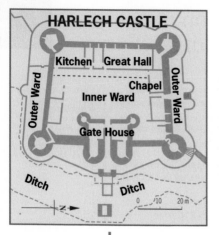

HARLECH CASTLE ✪✪✪

The dramatic location, high above the flat Harlech Morfa dunes give an extra dimension to this superbly preserved castle, which is also a UNESCO World Heritage Site. The views across the land reclaimed from the sea and across the mountains of Snowdonia are stunning.

The concept of the late 13th century castle is also fascinating. Because of its precipitous location, it seemed unnecessary to build double walls, and the architect thought that an extra-large gatehouse would suffice. However, the castle was not impregnable, as was demonstrated by the rebel Owain Glyndwr who captured it in 1404 and made it his headquarters. During the two later civil wars, Harlech fell into the hands of attackers on more than one occasion.

LLANBERIS ✪✪

The proximity of Snowdon (➤ 23, 43) has certainly not done this town any harm. Everyday large numbers of day trippers gather here to start the climb to the summit or to visit one of the tourist attractions.

Naturally, Llanberis has the necessary hotels, guest houses and places to eat and drink, and there is no shortage of souvenir shops.

The Llyn Padarn Country Park by the lake of the same name offers water-sports facilities, trails, picnic sites and craft shops. The Quarry Hospital Museum is also worthy, as is the Llanberis Lake Railway. You can interrupt your trip on this narrow-gauge railway halfway through the 4km (2.5-mile) journey to take in the Cwm Derwen Nature Centre.

The **Welsh Slate Museum** relates the story of slate and slate mining, an industry that once accounted for 3,000 jobs in the area. The **Electric Mountain** is also unusual. This is the Dinorwig hydroelectric power station, for which the world's largest man-made cave was hewn into the mountain. In size it is equivalent to two football fields and a 16-storey apartment block.

The cylindrical, 12m-high keep of the early-13th century Dolbadarn Castle, on the other hand, is more in harmony with the landscape. The location of this fortification, once the home of Llywelyn the Great, is particularly attractive; the painters Turner and Wilson certainly thought so.

✚ 28B4
☎ 01766 780552
🕐 Open daily, 9:30–4, 5 or 6 depending on the season
♿ Not all parts are accessible
💷 Moderate

✚ 28B4

Welsh Slate Museum
✉ Part of Llyn Padarn Country Park
☎ 01286 870630
🕐 Easter–Oct, daily 10–5; Nov–Easter, Sun–Fri 10–4
🍴 Café
♿ Very good
💷 Moderate

Electric Mountain
✉ On the ring road (A4086)
☎ 01286 870636
🕐 Jan–15 Mar, Thu–Sun 10:30–4:30; 15 Mar–Sep, daily 9:30–5:30; Oct–Dec, daily 10:30–5:30
🍴 Café at visitor centre
♿ Very good
💷 Visitor centre free, tour moderate
❓ Telephone reservations advisable in peak season in view of coach capacity

LLANDUDNO ✪✪

Regarded as the best seaside resort in northwest Wales, Llandudno owes its elegant, almost imposing appearance to its heyday as a health resort. In Victorian times, in particular, it was full of rich and eminent bathing guests, and many sights date from this period. Nevertheless, Llandudno is not a sleepy resort, dreaming of past glory. It is a lively town, which has managed to adapt to the modern age.

Its location is striking. The crescentic beach with its promenade lined with pale, stately hotels is confined by the capes of Little Ormes Head (142m) and Great Ormes Head (207m). The latter is the more prominent tourist attraction. It has acquired the status of a country park and it is possible to drive round it via the twisting Marine Drive (toll road). Pedestrians can use the Orme Nature Trail, the Victorian cable tram or the cableway. The starting point for all these is in the immediate vicinity of the Happy Valley Road, not far from the pier (1877).

At the top of Great Ormes Head is a visitor centre, a café and restaurant, and a copper mine whose history dates back some 4,000 years. Attractions in the town include the Alice in Wonderland Centre (Trinity Square), devoted to the adventures narrated in the famous book; the Oriel Mostyn Gallery (Vaughan Street), with a superb collection of international contemporary art; and the modern North Wales Theatre (Promenade), offering a range of top entertainments.

Thirteen kilometres (8 miles) south, in the Vale of Conwy, lies one of the most attractive gardens in Wales, the 40ha **Bodnant Garden**, set high above the River Conwy. From here there is a fine panorama of Snowdonia.

The 19th-century **Bodelwyddan Castle**, near St Asaph, houses 19th-century portraits on permanent loan from the London National Portrait Gallery, and works of art from the Victoria & Albert Museum and the Royal Academy.

✚ 29C5

Bodnant Garden
- ✉ 13km (8 miles) south on the A470
- ☎ 01492 650460
- 🕐 15 Mar–31 Oct, daily 10–5
- 🍴 Near car park
- 🚌 25 from Llandudno
- ♿ Excellent
- 💷 Moderate

Bodelwyddan Castle
- ✉ 24km (15 miles) east, on the A55 near St Asaph
- ☎ 01745 584060
- 🕐 Jul–Sep, daily 10–5; May–Jun, Oct, Sat–Thu 10–5; Oct–Apr, daily 10–3:30
- ♿ Very good
- 💷 Moderate

Cable cars take visitors up to Great Orme Country Park

Criccieth Castle
☎ 01766 522227
🕐 Apr–Sep, daily 10–4
♿ Good
💰 Cheap

THE LLEYN PENINSULA ✪✪

Protected as an Area of Outstanding Natural Beauty, the peninsula has a variety of landscapes. On the more populated south coast, tourism is the main source of income. Between Criccieth and Aberdaron there are plenty of beautiful sandy beaches for swimming and sunbathing, such as Abererch, the Warren near Llanbedrog and Aberdaron. The 5km-wide, almost deserted bay of Porth Neigwl (Hell's Mouth) is very popular with surfers, and the harbours of Pwllheli and Abersoch offer good moorings for yachts. Pwllheli, which more or less plays the role of capital of the area, is a fairly standard tourist resort. Abersoch has much more character and atmosphere, as has the modest fishing village of Aberdaron.

Inland the countryside is green and undulating, sparsely populated and largely agricultural. The landscape is satisfying, but never spectacular. Towards the southwest it becomes slightly less cultivated and more open in character. The Celtic language and culture have been well preserved in this fairly isolated area.

The north coast consists of an attractive combination of cliffs and small, secluded bays, such as Porthor (Porth Oer) and Porth Iago. The former is also called Whistling Sands Bay, as the dry sand makes a whistling sound when it is walked on. The hamlet of Porth Dinllaen further north is a real beauty spot. It can be reached only on foot across the beach or the golf course from Morfa Nefyn. The heights above the popular Ty Coch Inn provide a grand panorama across the bay.

*The sands between
Llanbedrog and
Abersoch*

The three peaks of Yr Eifl (maximum 564m) can be seen all around. They form the transition to the mountains of Snowdonia. On the eastern peak lie the remains of Tre'r Ceiri, the 'City of Giants', an Iron Age hill fort from the first century AD. A trip to the top is rewarded by a fine view.

Touring round the peninsula, you can break your journey at several tourist attractions or historic sights. The shingle beach of the small seaside resort of Criccieth is dominated by the impressive remains of **Criccieth Castle** on a small peninsula. This fortress was originally built in 1230, but received extra fortification from Edward I in the 1280s, during the construction of other Edwardian castles in north Wales.

In Llanystumdwy you can find the grave of the Liberal prime minister David Lloyd George (1863–1945), who spent his childhood in the village. There is also a museum dedicated to him. Still further west at a short distance from the main road stands Penarth Fawr, a 15th-century hall house. The road continues past Starcoast World, an enormous bungalow village with a theme park and an (excellently appointed) subtropical swimming pool.

Llanbedrog is home to a wonderful gallery of Welsh art in Plas Glyn-y-Weddw, while enthusiasts of religious art should visit the late medieval church of Llanengan, even if only to see the screen between the nave and the choir.

The 16th-century Plas yn Rhiw is a good example of a small Welsh manor house. Its ornamental gardens and grounds look out onto Cardigan Bay.

In the southwestern corner of the Lleyn Peninsula, the 160m Mynydd Mawr offers views across the coastline and Bardsey Island (Ynys Enlli). It is said that thousands of saints were buried on this island, which is why it was much visited by pilgrims. Now that it is a nature reserve, Bardsey has limited access and is visited mainly by birdwatchers.

Criccieth is a typical Welsh seaside town

28B4
01766 770000
Daily 9:30–5:30
Some parts accessible with difficulty
Moderate
Choice of shops in village

PORTMEIRION ✪✪

This private village built in Italian style provokes wide-ranging responses: the extravagant combination of some 50 pastel buildings, fake façades, columns, fountains, statues, a campanile, a piazza, and even a victory arch in different styles may seem to some an expression of poor taste or as misplaced in the surrounding area. However, most visitors react enthusiastically, especially perhaps if they enjoy theatrical architecture.

It took the architect Clough Williams-Ellis (1883–1978) several decades from 1925 to realise his dream – a new Portofino on British soil. The carefully chosen, secluded location makes it possible to grow tropical vegetation, which undoubtedly contributes to the Mediterranean character of the place. Visitors have to leave their cars outside the village.

Sir Clough Williams-Ellis's Italianate village of Portmeirion is modelled on Portofino

TYWYN ✪✪

Tywyn (The Strand) is a typical seaside town with 5km (3 miles) of sandy beach and a fascinating hinterland. Those who wish to explore the luscious Talyllyn valley can go by miniature steam train along the 11km (7-mile) narrow-gauge Talyllyn Railway dating from 1865. You can break your journey on the steam train en route and take a walk – through the woods to the Dolgoch Falls, for example.

Perhaps even more beautiful and certainly more remote is the Dysynni Valley further north, dominated to the east by the foothills of Cader Idris. The 13th-century Castell y Bere of the Welsh princes is one of the most beautifully situated castle ruins. Another stunning feature is the 233m-high Craig yr Aderyn (Birds' Rock), a breeding place for cormorants.

A Drive through Snowdonia

This tour is a good introduction to the mountains and valleys of the northern part of the Snowdonia National Park. It is advisable to allow a full day for it.

The starting point is the mountain village of Beddgelert (▶ 33). Take the A498 northeastwards up Nantgwynant.

After passing Llyn Dinas and Llyn Gwynant, you will see a car park high up on the left. The views from here across Nantgwynant are magnificent.

Turn left on to the A4086 and follow it through the Pass of Llanberis.

In Llanberis you can break your journey for a climb to the top of Snowdon (▶ 23), which can also be reached by mountain train. Llanberis itself has a number of sights (▶ 38).

The B4547, B4366 and B4409 make the link with the slate village of Bethesda (▶ 34), after which the ascent through Nant Ffrancon begins via the A5.

On the top of the mountain pass you can visit the Ogwen Falls and the Cwm Idwal nature reserve.

The A5 follows the course of the Llugwy via the mountaineering village of Capel Curig to the tourist resort of Betws–y–coed.

Betws-y-coed is especially famous for its beautiful surroundings and many waterfalls (▶ 34).

The A470 leads southwest to Blaenau Ffestiniog (▶ 35) high in the mountains, and passes the medieval tower of Dolwyddelan Castle with its wonderful views.

The Llechwedd Slate Caverns and the Ffestiniog Railway (▶ 19) are the main attractions in Blaenau.

The route back to the start point is via the A496, A487, B4410 and the A4085.

Distance
120km (75 miles)

Start/end point
Beddgelert
➕ 28B4

Lunch (depending on start point)
Llanberis, Betws-y-coed

Get out of the car and admire the beautiful landscape

Central Wales

Much of central Wales is a sparsely populated, year-round green region of hills, forests and lakes. Narrow, twisting mountain roads lead through the Cambrian Mountains across imposing mountain passes and cloudy heights, past long reservoirs to small villages with unpronounceable names.

Along the coast there is only one town of any importance: the Victorian seaside resort of Aberystwyth. To the south, views are dominated by the Brecon Beacons National Park, an extensive massif of flat mountain tops, criss-crossed by narrow river valleys.

The eastern border region, the fertile basin of rivers such as the Dee, the Severn and the Wye, is the most cultivated. The influence of its English neighbours is clearly noticeable here.

> *' Their Lord they shall praise,*
> *Their language they shall keep,*
> *Their land they shall lose,*
> *Except Wild Wales. '*

TALIESIN
6th-century British bard

———————•———————

Left: *the ruins of Castell y Bere in the Dysynni Valley*

✚ 28B3

Llanerchaeron

✉ 4km (2.5 miles) east on the A482

☎ 01545 570200

🕐 Apr–Oct, Thu–Sun 11–5

🚌 202
Carmarthen–Aberaeron

♿ Excellent

💷 Cheap

ABERAERON   ⭐⭐

This town is predominantly Georgian in character and owes its harmonious look to Reverend Alban Gwynne and his wife. These two early 19th-century benefactors paid for the restoration and extension of the town and harbour out of their own pockets. Their intervention can still be considered a success, as Aberaeron is a charming resort with colourful buildings surrounding a grid of streets, squares and the harbour.

Visitors mooring their boats in the marina or making a short stop will find plenty to see: a sea aquarium, bee exhibition, craft workshops and a manual air gondola above the Aeron river. Just outside the town there is a zoo with theme park (3km/2 miles northeast via the A487), a vineyard (beyond the built-up area in the direction of Lampeter), and the elegant **Llanerchaeron**, built in classical style. This 18th-century house, by John Nash, is being renovated but the landscaped park and gardens can be visited.

✚ 29D2

ABERGAVENNY (Y FENNI)   ⭐

Apart from the 14th-century church there is little in this prosperous market town which is an absolute must. If you happen to be passing, you can see the busy cattle market on a Tuesday (the general market is on Friday), and there are also good opportunities for walks in the vicinity. The high mountain peaks such as the Blorenge (552m), Sugar Loaf (596m), and Skirrid Fawr (486m) can be climbed and offer the reward of a good view from the summit.

ABERYSTWYTH ✪

Aberystwth is a traditional British seaside resort, both in appearance and its amusement facilities. The beach (sand and shingle) is bordered by a long promenade with stately Victorian hotels and pier. On the north side, an electric tram from 1896 takes you to the 130m Constitution Hill, which offers clear views of the curving bay. There is also a camera obscura here, a typically 19th-century attraction.

🚩 28B3
ℹ️ Terrace Road
☎ 01970 612125

National Library of Wales
✉️ Penglais Hill
☎ 01970 632800/623834
🕐 Mon–Fri 9:30–6,
Sat 9:30–5
💷 Free
♿ Good

The Victorian buildings of Aberystwyth University

The other side of the seafront is dominated by the neo-Gothic main building of the university. Most of Wales's oldest academy has since moved to a modern campus on Penglais Hill, which contains the Arts Centre (including a theatre) as well as the **National Library of Wales** with its valuable collection of manuscripts.

The late-13th century Aberystwyth Castle is very fragmentary after its demolition in 1649. The adjacent St Michael's Church shows the history of the Christian faith in Wales while the city museum is splendidly housed in the former Coliseum (music hall and cinema). In the suburb of Llanbadarn Fawr stands a large early 13th-century church with two Celtic crosses, which are among the tallest in Wales.

🔢 29C2

ℹ️ Mountain Centre Libanus (8km/5 miles southwest of Brecon, on the A470). Visitor centres in Abergavenny (Monmouth Road), Brecon (Cattle Market car park), Llandovery (Kings Road) and the Craig-y-nos Country Park

The Brecon Beacons are perfect horse-riding country

BRECON BEACONS NATIONAL PARK ✪✪✪

The national park (1,344sq km) was founded in 1957, the tenth in a series which has since unofficially increased to twelve. The Brecon Beacons consist mainly of four mountain tops, formed by red sandstone 345 to 395 million years old. This largely treeless series of hills is cut by river valleys, invariably running from north to south. In addition, there are 18 reservoirs and extensive forests, most of which have been planted by the Forestry Commission.

From east to west you can distinguish the following ranges: the Black Mountains (where the 811m Waun Fach is the main peak), the Brecon Beacons (with the 886m Pen y Fan, the highest mountain in south Wales), the Fforest Fawr (with the 726m Gyhirych), and the irregularly shaped Black Mountain (Fan Brycheiniog, 802m), which is in fact a range of peaks.

Visitors setting out by car will be able to enjoy only part of the rugged natural beauty of the park. Only on foot it is possible to experience the peace of the sometimes barren moorlands and the solitary tops. The most popular route to a summit is the path from the A470 (Pont ar Daf, south of Storey Arms) to Pen y Fan. An alternative path, which is more impressive for its landscape but more difficult to negotiate, winds its way from the Upper Neuadd Reservoir to the summit.

The walk from Llanddeusant in the heart of the Black Mountain to the lakes of Llyn y Fan Fach and Llyn y Fan Fawr is also beautiful.

The ruins of Llanthony Priory now include an inn

The slopes and valleys of the eastern Black Mountains are suitable for less trained walkers: for example, the Vale of Ewyas (▶ 26), where Llanthony is a good starting place, or the valley of the Grwyne Fawr from Patrishow. Or you can walk along the Monmouthshire and Brecon Canal, across Mynydd Llangorse above the lake of the same name, through the Talybont Forest and the adjacent forests of Taf Fechan, on the path from Ystradfellte along the Mellte river with its many waterfalls , and in the Craig-y-nos Country Park.

Horse riding is possible around Brecon, in the Usk Valley, and in the Vale of Ewyas. Llangorse Lake, the Wye near Glasbury, and the Usk near Brecon Promenade, respectively, are suitable for sailing and canoeing.

The roads that cut through the national park from north to south provide a good impression of the area and some magnificent views. As the roads are fairly busy, the solitary and deserted character of the region is slightly lost here. This is why the narrow road from Heol Senni to Ystradfellte is a much better choice, as is the narrow route through the Vale of Ewyas.

Although the Brecon Beacons National Park is the domain of sports enthusiasts and nature lovers, there are historical remains and larger tourist attractions. Carreg Cennen Castle (▶ 50) with its unsurpassed location and the evocative ruins of Llanthony Priory (▶ 26) are two musts. Tretower Court is a fine, fortified manor from the 15th century, which has been largely preserved (▶ 52); nearby stands the 13th-century cylindrical keep of an earlier Norman castle. Also worth a visit are the churches of Brecon (cathedral), Patrishow, Cwmyoy, Llanelieu and Llywel. Crickhowell, with its 16th-century bridge, is a most charming small town.

The Brecon Mountain Railway (3km/2 miles north of Merthyr Tydfil), the Dan-yr-Ogof caves and Dinosaur Park (near Craig-y-nos), and the Brecknock Museum in Brecon with its large collection of love spoons are some of the tourist attractions within the national park's boundaries.

Right: *Cardigan Church*

 28A2

Cilgerran Castle
✉ In Cilgerran, via the A478
☎ 01239 615007
🕐 Apr–Oct, daily 9:30–6:30; Nov–Mar, 9:30–4
🍴 In village
🚌 430 from Cardigan (3–5 a day)
♿ Ground level accessible
 Cheap

Welsh Wildlife Centre
✉ South of Cardigan via the A478
☎ 01239 621600
🕐 Easter–Oct, daily from 10:30
🍴 Tearoom
🚌 430 from Cardigan (3–5 a day)
♿ Good
 Fairly moderate

✚ 28B2
✉ Minor road from the A483 to Trapp
☎ 01558 822291
🕐 Apr–Oct, 9:30–6:30; Nov–Mar, 9:30–sunset
🍴 Café
🚋 Ffairfach, 6.5km (4 miles) northwest
♿ Not suitable Cheap

CARDIGAN (ABERTEIFI) ⭐

A friendly, lively town with a long high street, flanked by a colourful variety of shops, cafés and inns. Behind the neo-Gothic Guildhall is the covered market, where fresh produce is sold. The Theatre Mwldan (▶ 111) is a centre of cultural life, drawing visitors from afar.

Little remains of Cardigan Castle, which was founded in the 11th century. The fragmentary ruins look out on to the Teifi Bridge (1726). The first recorded eisteddfod was held in the fortress for Rhys ap Gruffydd in 1179.

There are many sights around Cardigan. In St Dogmaels (Llandudoch) there are remains of a 12th- century Benedictine monastery. Opposite is the Y-Felin watermill, which is still in use.

The ruins of **Cilgerran Castle** (13th century), once painted by Turner, mainly consist of two massive towers, which dominate the Teifi Valley. Between Cilgerran and Cardigan is the 109ha **Welsh Wildlife Centre**, one of the best zoos in the principality.

Cenarth, also on the Teifi, is well known for its waterfall, which is in fact a series of rapids. The adjacent National Coracle Centre housed in a 17th-century watermill features the coracles. These oval-shaped one-man boats are made of wooden slats covered by hide or canvas. The annual coracle race takes place in August.

CARREG CENNEN CASTLE ⭐⭐⭐

The main impression of this castle, dating from about 1300, is its dramatic location on a steep 100m-high limestone crag. After changing ownership several times between the English and the Welsh, the fortress fell into the hands of a gang of robbers in the 15th century. When these had eventually been chased away, it was decided to dismantle the castle though much remains standing. The 45m-long cliff tunnel is a remarkable feature. In the neighbouring village of Trapp is a craft centre.

A Walk along the Ceredigion Heritage Coast

New Quay (Ceinewydd) is a picturesque seaside town whose predominantly white houses are built in terraces on a slope. Most shops, pubs and restaurants are situated in the bustling Lower Town.

The coast path, which offers splendid views, runs via New Quay Head and Birds Rock (breeding place for birds) to Cwmtydu, an isolated ravine between high, green slopes, which once served as a pirates' nest and smugglers' den. The path then continues towards Ynys–Lochtyn and the cosy village of Llangranog.

Ynys-Lochtyn is a small rugged cape and island. Llangranog, with its two sandy beaches, nestles between steep green slopes, and in summer is very popular with day trippers.

The coast path winds its way along other bays with beautiful beaches, such as the spacious Treath Penbryn, which is suitable for children, and the secluded beach at Tresaith, popular with water-sports enthusiasts. Then Aberporth comes into view.

Aberporth is a friendly town with two sandy beaches and good facilities. It is a fairly quiet place, but popular with the Welsh.

The landscape remains impressive as you start the last section. On the way to Cardigan, a visit to Mwnt is a must.

Mwnt headland is a real beauty spot, with a small ravine and cliffs covered in grass and ferns. At the top stands a simple white 15th-century church. In the summer it can be busy here.

Distance
35km (22 miles)

Time
8–10 hours (without long breaks)

Start point
New Quay
✚ Not on the map; 30km (19 miles) northeast of Cardigan

End point
Cardigan
✚ 28A2
🚌 550
Aberystwyth–Aberaeron–New Quay–Tresaith–Aberporth–Cardigan and return

Lunch and tea
Llangrannog (more places to eat and drink), Tresaith

Stopover
Aberporth: Hotel Penrallt (£££) and Highcliffe Hotel (££)

The limewashed church of Mwnt dates from the Middle Ages

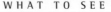

 29C2

Tretower Court and Castle

✉ 5km (3 miles) northwest via the A40/A479

☎ 01874 730279

🕐 10–4, 5 or 6, depending on the season

♿ Not all parts are accessible

🎫 Cheap

CRICKHOWELL (CINCYWELL) ⭐⭐

This attractive town in the wide Usk Valley has a good choice of historic inns and is an excellent place to linger. The Porth Mawr (Large Gate) is 14th century, as is the parish church; the bridge dates from the 16th and 17th centuries, while the houses and shops in Bridge Street are Georgian in style.

A climb up the 451m Table Mountain to the north, with traces of the Iron Age fort of Crug Hywel on the summit, gains a superb view of Crickhowell and the surrounding area. The Craig y Cilian Nature Reserve with its caves and rock formations is another good excursion; it is not far from Llangattock. Historic Patrishow Church and **Tretower Court** (▶ 49) are also nearby.

✚ 29C3

The triple bridge at Devil's Bridge

DEVIL'S BRIDGE (PONTARFYNACH) ⭐⭐

This is a busy, sometimes crowded village at the end of the beautiful Vale of Rheidol. The name refers to the 12th-century bridge across the Mynach built by monks from Strata Florida Abbey (▶ 52).

A new bridge, also made of stone, was built above the medieval bridge in 1753, and a third bridge made of iron was added in 1901.

For a good view of the three bridges it is best to go down into the more than 90m-deep, densely wooded ravine (small entrance fee). A short walk via Jacob's Ladder with its hundred steps leads to Devil's Bridge or Mynach Falls, close to the spot where the Mynach and Rheidol rivers come together.

There are other attractive waterfalls that can be visited on pleasant trails, and it is also possible to take a trip on the Vale of Rheidol Railway. Drivers may take the B4574 southeast to the lonely village of Cwmystwyth, and then go east towards the Elan Valley. This road provides an introduction to the wild mountain region of central Wales.

The Dolaucothi Gold Mines can be explored with a guide

ELAN VALLEY ✪✪

➕ 29C3

The 'lake district of central Wales', as this area is sometimes called, consists of five reservoirs. Four of these were built between 1892 and 1903 for the city of Birmingham, nearly 120km (75 miles) east; the fifth dates from 1952. The total capacity of the lakes – which stretch for 14km (9 miles) – is more than 100,000 million litres of water. Building them in this watershed area was highly controversial and led to fierce protests; hardly surprising, as more than a thousand inhabitants had to make way for reservoirs serving an English city.

At the Caban Coch dam the information centre describes the creation and function of the reservoirs, the local flora and wildlife, and the various opportunities for walking and cycling. These include the Elan Valley Trail and the mountain paths of Claerwen to the Teifi Pools and Strata Florida Abbey.

A 24km (15-mile) tour along the four original reservoirs allows the driver or cyclist to explore a combination of woods, lakes, moors and dams. The dams were given ornate buildings, according to the fashion of the time.

LAMPETER (LLANBEDR PONT STEFFAN) ✪

➕ 28B2

In 1822 this modest town on the Teifi became home to the first university college of Wales, with an aim of providing higher education for young people from unprivileged backgrounds in the area. This establishment and Lampeter's role as a regional centre ensured the town's long-term development. Lampeter offers a good choice of traditional inns, modern bistros, student pubs and shops.

Near Pumpsaint on the A482 to Llanwrda are the **Dolaucothi Gold Mines** founded by the Romans. There are guided tours, some of which go underground.

Dolaucothi Gold Mines
✉ 13km (8 miles) southeast at Pumpsaint
☎ 011558 650359
🕐 Mid-Apr to mid-Sep, daily 10–5
🍴 Tearoom
♿ Guided tour not suitable for children under five
 Cheap

Food & Drink

British cuisine has improved over the last few decades. With careful choosing, you can now find excellent food and a variety of cuisines in Wales as elsewhere in the British Isles.

It is not always cheap to eat out in Britain, although there are variations in price and value. You should be prepared to pay for quality. Yet even in most pubs and inns you can have a good lunch or dinner for relatively little. Moreover, there is a pleasant informal atmosphere in these traditional eating and drinking places.

Taste of Wales

Restaurants, inns, pubs, guest houses, farms and tearooms that are members of the Taste of Wales (Blas ar Cymru) organisation founded in 1991 are of a guaranteed standard. Its members pledge to prepare meals with care, emphasising the use of fresh and, whenever possible, local or regional ingredients. They also ensure quality service. A Taste of Wales establishment can be recognised by the red dragon logo. Tourist offices have lists of Taste of Wales members.

Fish and chips remains one of the most popular dishes in Wales as in the rest of Britain

Welsh Cuisine

Lamb, beef and many kinds of fish (salmon, trout, crab, lobster, cockles, sea bass, halibut) are the most prominent

Laver bread (bara lawr) is typically Welsh and is often served at breakfast

ingredients of Welsh cuisine. Because the working population once consisted mostly of fishermen and farmers, and later also of miners and factory workers, dishes were often simple but filling. Moreover, there was a preference for local meat and staple ingredients (potatoes, carrots, leeks, cabbage). This is how the well-known stews and soups came into being, such as Welsh lamb hot pot and cawl.

Roast beef is often on the menu

Of course, there are also lighter dishes on the Welsh menu. There is fresh trout wrapped in ham or bacon and other more curious dishes such as bara lawr (laver bread), made from seaweed and oatmeal. The best-known dish is perhaps also the simplest: Welsh rarebit, melted cheese on toast (► 95).

There are dozens of Welsh cheeses, such as the mild white Caerphilly and Pencarreg, nicknamed Welsh Brie, but also more local types such as Caws Coch Llyn and Caws Ffermdy Cenarth.

Baking

The baking plate and baking stone have always been widely used in Welsh cuisine. They are used not only for pancakes, but also for bara brith, a firm loaf containing dried fruit that has been soaked in tea (► 94), and Welsh cakes, flat scone-like cakes cooked on a griddle.

Markets
Open-air markets can be found in every town of any significance. In the big cities there are also daily covered markets, such as in Cardiff, Carmarthen (only Wednesday and Saturday), Haverfordwest, Newport (Gwent), Swansea and Wrexham.

Wales has its own brands and types of beer

+ 28B2

Dinefwr Park
- ✉ On the western edge of Llandeilo
- ☎ 01558 823902
- 🕐 Apr–Oct, Thu–Mon 11–4:30
- 🍴 Tearoom
- 🚉 Llandeilo
- 💷 Cheap

Above: *Tywi Valley near Llandeilo*

+ 29C2

LLANDEILO ✪✪

The predominantly Victorian houses of this small, friendly town are concentrated around a number of narrow streets. There are no particular striking buildings, with the exception of the long, 111m-high bridge (1848) across the Tywi. This makes the area around the town all the more fascinating.

Within walking distance is **Dinefwr Park**, a magnificent landscaped estate, which includes the castle perched on a rock above high the river. It was founded in the 12th century by Lord Rhys and is surrounded by the 25ha Castle Woods Nature Reserve. Around 1660, Newton House was built to replace the dilapidated fortress. In the 19th century the country mansion was given a Gothic facelift. Prior to that, in 1775, it had been framed by a grand landscaped park, the domain of deer and cattle.

Nearby, south of the B4300, is the Gelli Aur Country Park, a 36ha wooded estate with terraced gardens and an arboretum. The beautifully located 13th-century Dryswlyn Castle, which has fine views, was built by Welsh princes to guard the Tywi Valley. This area also boasts the National Botanic Garden of Wales (▶ 20) and the dramatically situated ruin of Carreg Cennen Castle (▶ 50).

LLANDOVERY (LLANYMDDYFRI) ✪

There is to disturb the peace little in this somewhat sleepy, Welsh market town , excepting the weekly cattle market (Tuesdays). But the 19th-century writer, George Borrow, thought it 'the pleasantest little town in which I have halted'. The cobbled market place, the clock tower, the inns and the Georgian facades have given the place a certain historic charm, although little or nothing remains of the oldest buildings (a Roman fort and a medieval castle). The Dinefwr Craft Centre sells local products. Otherwise, the town provides a favourable base in relation to excursions to central Wales and the Brecon Beacons National Park (▶ 48).

LLANDRINDOD WELLS ✪

 29C3

The expansion of the railways in the mid-19th century and the discovery of therapeutic waters turned this insignificant town into a bustling Victorian health resort. There are many reminders of this period in the public buildings and architecture of some of the districts, the luscious Rock Park Gardens with the restored Pump Room in the Spa Centre, and several hotels and theatres. There are a number of small museums, specialising in the town's history and in bicycles, for example. In addition, there are various sports facilities, ranging from golf, tennis, bowling and angling to boating on an artificial lake. And finally, the town of Llandrindod hosts special festivities such as an annual eisteddfod and the Victorian Festival. It plays a central role in a beautiful if unspectacular area of woods and robust farmland.

The townsfolk of Llandrindod Wells dress up for the Victorian Festival each August

LLANWRTYD WELLS ✪

29C2

This small town is situated in beautiful surroundings in the green valley of the Irfon. In Victorian times it was a popular health resort, attracting visitors from the industrialised regions of south Wales. The therapeutic spring waters rich in sulphate are no longer available and only the Victorian architecture reveals the town's former role as a spa.

Nevertheless, Llanwrtyd still draws visitors. They come for the beautiful woods, the excellent horse-riding and mountain-biking facilities, and for the extensive calendar of events, which includes the Man versus Horse Marathon, the Four-Day Walks, the Four-Day Cycle Race and the Mid-Wales Beer Festival. At the Cambrian Woollen Mill you can watch a demonstration of the production process.

The 22km (14-mile) drive across the Abergwesyn Pass to Tregaron (▶ 59) is a good introduction to the moorlands known as the Roof of Wales and the Green Desert.

29C2

LLYN BRIANNE

This enormous reservoir built in the early 1970s for the city of Swansea lies in a remote area. The road along the eastern shore (►59) shadows the full extent and irregular shape of this lake fed by the Twyi and Camddwr rivers.

The densely wooded western side of Llyn Brianne can be explored only on foot, for example from the dam at the southern end. Nearby to the south is the Dinas Hill Nature Reserve. This area is one of the last breeding places of the rare red kite. Among the other birds of prey found here is the buzzard.

 29B3

Celtica
- ☒ Y Plas, in the centre
- ☎ 01654 702702
- ◷ Daily 10–6. Closed Christmas
- 🍴 Tearoom
- ♿ Very good
- 💷 Moderate

Centre for Alternative Technology
- ☒ 4km (2.5 miles) north via the A487
- ☎ 01654 702400
- ◷ Summer, daily 10–5:30; hols, daily 9:30–6; winter, daily 10–4. Closed Christmas and January
- 🍴 Restaurant
- 🚌 Bus from Machynlleth
- ♿ Good 💷 Moderate

MACHYNLLETH

A friendly town with a wide high street, dominated by the clock tower of 1873. This ornate building was donated by a local nobleman, the Marquess of Londonderry. His house, the elegant 17th century Plas Machynlleth, now houses **Celtica**, an exhibition featuring Celtic history and culture.

Parliament House is a reminder of the Welsh struggle for independence. In 1404 the rebel Owain Glyndwr summoned a Welsh parliament here. In the 1950s, this event inspired Machynlleth to claim (in vain) its status as capital of Wales. The Owain Glyndwr Centre in the town pays ample tribute to this hero.

An old chapel, Y Tabernacl, houses the Wales Museum of Modern Art. Besides its contemporary art collection, the museum also hosts cultural events. The **Centre for Alternative Technology**, founded in 1975 in the wooded area of a deserted slate quarry, explores various ecological subjects in a sympathetic way, with an emphasis on self-sufficiency. It is now one of Wales's major attractions.

 29C3

STRATA FLORIDA ABBEY

This Cistercian abbey founded in 1164 is one of the many monastic ruins in the principality. During the 12th and 13th centuries it became the centre of the country's religious, political, educational and cultural life. It is a beautiful and historic spot, but relatively little remains of the buildings themselves. The former western entrance to the church, in Romanesque style, is the best preserved feature and there is a small exhibition about the site.

Above: The wooded shoreline of Llyn Brianne

A Drive through the Cambrian Mountains

A mountain tour that introduces you to the southern part of the hilly, sparsely populated heart of Wales.

From the market town of Llandovery (➤ 56) a narrow, twisting road follows the Tywi north to the hamlet of Rhandirmwyn and then via the Dinas Hill bird reserve to the impressive dam on the south side of Llyn Brianne (➤ 58).

The road offers beautiful views as it winds its way along the eastern shore of the reservoir surrounded by conifers, and then climbs towards the barren upland plain.

The small town of Tregaron is reached via lonely mountain roads that cut across the Cambrian Mountains.

This remote town has a remarkably spacious market square, where cattle drivers used to gather their cows before taking them on the drovers' road via the Abergwesyn pass to the border with England. The Welsh Gold Centre is a craft shop specialising in jewellery with Celtic designs.

The B4343 then winds its way through an alternately open and densely wooded landscape of hills at a short distance from Strata Florida Abbey (➤ 58) towards Cwmystwyth. It is possible to make a small detour via Devil's Bridge (➤ 52). Now you cross the Cambrian Mountains again, this time via the lonely mountain road towards the Elan Valley (➤ 53). The trip then continues through 'the lake district of Wales' to the B4518 and the town of Rhayader.

If you wish to return to Llandovery, it is best to take the A470, B4358 and then the A483.

Distance
120km (75 miles) to Rhayader
170km (106 miles) round trip

Time
Full day

Start point
Llandovery
✠ 29C2

End point
Rhayader
✠ 29C3

Lunch
Rhandirmwyn (Royal Oak)
Tregaron (Talbot Hotel)
Devil's Bridge (Hafod Arms)

Strata Florida Abbey: remains of the Romanesque façade

Southwest Wales

Southwest Wales is largely taken up by the Pembrokeshire Coast National Park, a stunning combination of bays, gorges, ravines, cliffs, peninsulas, islands, caves, beaches and rock formations.

Included within the park are the windy, almost treeless Mynydd Preseli (Preseli Hills).

Four islands off the coast are home to large numbers of breeding waterbirds. Birds can be seen closer at hand in the Daugleddau estuary, the flat and peaceful basin of Milford Haven, its several tributaries reaching far inland.

Southwest Wales is rich in heritage too: there are beautiful churches, impressive castles, Celtic crosses and many prehistoric remains. And of course there are the places that tourists naturally enjoy – the sea and the beach.

> *'The Welsh go to extremes in all matters. You may never find anyone worse than a bad Welshman, but you will certainly never find anyone better than a good one.'*

GIRALDUS CAMBRENSIS (GERALD OF WALES),
from his account of his trip around Wales in 1188

———————————●———————————

Left: *the Elegug Stacks are a well known feature of the Pembrokeshire coast*

Carew Castle and French Mill
☎ 01646 651782
🕐 Easter–Oct, daily 10–5
🍴 Pub and restaurant in village
♿ Partially accessible
💷 Cheap

✚ 28A1

CAREW (CAERIW) ⭐⭐

If only a village, Carew does have a castle, a famous Celtic cross and a watermill. The ruins of **Carew Castle** present a picturesque setting on the shores of the Carew River, which widens here into a tributary of Milford Haven and as such is subject to the tides. The original Norman fortification was later renovated in Tudor and Elizabethan times, but sadly it is now an empty shell.

Carew Cross (▶ 5), dates from the early 11th century and is beautifully decorated. It was made and inscribed in honour of Maredudd ap Edwin, lord of Dyfed, who perished in battle about 1035.

The **Carew French Mill** originally dates from the 16th century, but the present four-storey building is mainly 19th century.

✚ 28A2

GWAUN VALLEY (CWM GWAUN) ⭐⭐⭐

A narrow, densely wooded valley with its own peculiar atmosphere, southeast of Llanychaer and Pontfaen, and accessible on minor roads that link with the B4313. The isolated character of the valley, with its rich flora and wildlife and excellent opportunities for walking and cycling, is illustrated by the fact that its inhabitants – albeit as a curiosity – keep to a pre-1752 Julian calendar, whereby the New Year starts on 13 January.

Time move slowly in the Gwaun Valley

KIDWELLY (CYDWELI) ⚙️⚙️

The dominant position of **Kidwelly Castle**, high above the Gwendraeth river, undoubtedly contributes to its impressive character. This fortress is less well known than the contemporary Edwardian castles in the north of the country and it is therefore recommended as one of Wales's best-kept secrets. The almost complete walls date from the late 13th century and the solid gatehouse from 1422. A 14th-century bridge crosses the river to St Mary's Church, the only surviving part of a priory founded in about 1130.

DID YOU KNOW?

Manorbier Castle (🟧 28A1) is where the historian Giraldus de Barri (Giraldus Cambrensis or Gerald of Wales) was born in about 1146. The account of his 965km (600-mile), 51-day trip around the principality in 1188, to accompany Archbishop Baldwin of Canterbury to preach and recruit for the Third Crusade is still one of the foremost sources on Wales in the Middle Ages.

LAUGHARNE (TALACHARN) ⚙️⚙️

This pleasant small town on the Taf estuary is especially known for its association with Wales's best-known poet, Dylan Thomas (▶ 14). But even without that it would be worth a visit. By the sea stands a picturesque castle ruin (May–Sep 10–17), which was once painted by Turner. The gardens in Georgian and Victorian style are currently being restored. You can visit the beautifully situated **boathouse** on the estuary, where Thomas lived. The flimsy outbuilding where the poet worked can be viewed only from the outside. A simple white cross in St Martin's churchyard marks the poet's grave.

🟧 28B1

Kidwelly Castle
✉️ In the town
☎️ 01554 890104
🕐 Jun–Sep, daily 9:30–6;
   Apr–May, Oct, daily
   9:30–5:30; Nov–Mar,
   Mon–Sat 9:30–4, Sun
   11–4. Closed Christmas
   and New Year
🚉 Kidwelly
♿ Good; partly accessible
💷 Cheap

Above: *the ruins of
Laugharne Castle
overlooking the Taf
estuary*

🟧 28B1

Dylan Thomas Boathouse
✉️ On the shore of the Taf in
   Laugharne
☎️ 01994 427420
🕐 May–Oct, 10–5; Nov–Apr,
   10:30–3
🍴 Tearoom
🚌 222 from Carmarthen
♿ Not suitable
💷 Cheap

In the Know

If you only have a short time to visit Wales, or would like to get a real flavour of the country, here are some ideas:

Remarkable towns and villages

Aberdaron. A typical Welsh town in an isolated position at the far end of the Lleyn Peninsula with a beautiful church, lovely cottages and sandy beach.

Beddgelert. Mountain village with cottages of local stone around a bridge, in the heart of Snowdonia.

Crickhowell. Historic town on the Usk with many historic buildings, including some excellent inns.

Laugharne. An attractive village, not only because of its memories of the writer Dylan Thomas, but also because of the historic high street, river and castle.

Llangrannog. White cottages and inns look out on to a small bay, which lies between the fern- and broom-covered slopes of the Ceredigion coast.

Llansteffan. An unpretentious, friendly village, dominated by a strategically located castle.

Montgomery. Charming town with Georgian buildings and a romantic castle ruin.

Porth Dinllaen. Hamlet in beautiful location on the north coast of the Lleyn Peninsula. It can be reached only on foot across the beach.

64

Solva. The small harbour of this picturesque village, so popular with watersports enthusiasts, lies at the end of a deep inlet surrounded by green hills.

Ystradfellte. Time seems to have stood still in this hamlet surrounded by the impressive natural beauty of the Brecon Beacons. Altogether not much more than a church, pub and a few houses.

Best-preserved castles

- Beaumaris
- Caerphilly
- Caernarfon
- Chepstow
- Conwy
- Criccieth
- Harlech
- Kidwelly
- Pembroke
- Raglan

Impressive country houses

- Castell Coch
- Chirk Castle
- Erddig
- Penhow Castle
- Penrhyn Castle
- Plas Newydd (Llangollen)
- Plas Newydd (Anglesey)
- Plas Yn Rhiw
- Powis Castle
- Tredegar

Beauty spots

Bwlch y Groes Pass. This road over the Llantysilio Mountain near Llangollen is one of the most breathtaking in Wales.

Carreg Cennen Castle. Wales's most evocative ruin, dramatically situated on a high rock in the Black Mountain range.

Castell y Bere. The weathered remains of this Welsh castle give a human dimension to the idyllic and verdant Dysynni Valley.

Cwm Idwal. This glacial valley with a lake near Bethesda is surrounded

The Glaslyn flows through the mountain village of Beddgelert

by rugged, steep slopes, and was Wales's first nature reserve. It can be reached on foot from the west of Llyn Ogwen.

Cwm Nantcol and **Cwm Bychan.** Two easily accessible narrow valleys, east of Llanbedr. The latter leads to a solitary lake and the so-called Roman Steps, part of a road of medieval origin.

Llyn y Fan Fach and **Llyn y Fan Fawr** are two mountain lakes which are characteristic of the Brecon Beacons and accessible via a stunning, but taxing mountain walk from Llanddeusant.

Nantgwynant. A luscious valley with two lakes, framed by the mountains of Snowdonia.

South Stack. Rock cape protruding into the sea. Fantastic view, a lighthouse and a bird observation post on the west side of Holy Island (Anglesey).

Threecliffs Bay. The most attractive bay of Gower, accessible only on foot from Parkmill.

Worms Head. A narrow headland stretching in to the sea at the western end of Gower. Accessible on foot via a causeway that floods at high tide.

Fascinating museums

Big Pit Mining Museum. Coal mine closed in 1980. Underground tour reveals authentic mine shafts.

Blaenavon Ironworks. This World Heritage Site confirms the importance of south Wales in the Industrial Revolution – Welsh heritage writ large.

Bodelwyddan Castle. Victorian country house, serving as a branch of the London National Portrait Gallery.

Caerleon Fortress Baths. Important excavation of a bathhouse complex from Roman times.

Ceredigion Museum, Aberystwyth. Regional museum housed in a beautiful old music hall,

Llyn Gwynant is an idyllic spot in Snowdonia

one of the best of its kind.

Llechwedd Slate Caverns. Not to be missed if you want an impression of the slate quarries that have been so important to the economy of northwest Wales.

Museum of Welsh Life. *The* open-air museum in Wales, with a collection of traditional buildings. In St Fagan's near Cardiff.

National Museum and Gallery. Many facets of the principality are displayed in Cardiff's most important museum.

Swansea Maritime and Industrial Museum. The maritime and industrial history of Wales's second city is the focus of this museum.

Techniquest. Science and engineering are illustrated by practical examples in this museum in Cardiff Bay. The museum is fun for both children and adults.

28A2

PRESELI HILLS (MYNYDD PRESELI) ⬤⬤

At a height of some 500m these broad hills covered with heather and grass together form a long and windy plateau with a remarkable number of prehistoric remains. The most important is undoubtedly the 5,500-year-old neolithic chamber tomb of Pentre Ifan, which is constructed with the Preseli bluestones as used at Stonehenge. Carreg Coetan, a younger version of Pentre Ifan, is also worth visiting, as are a number of hill forts and settlements from the Iron Age, such as Castell Henllys (a contemporary reconstruction).

Pentre Ifan is the best-known prehistoric monument in Pembrokeshire

The engaging village of Nevern has a ruined castle on a hill, old cottages, a medieval bridge and a historic parish church in a mixture of Romanesque and Gothic styles, with a 4m-high, 10th-century Celtic cross in the atmospheric churchyard.

 28A1

Pembroke Castle
☎ 01646 681510
🕒 Apr–Sep, 9:30–6; Mar, Oct 10–5; Nov–Feb 10–4
♿ Reasonable
🎟 Moderate

PEMBROKE (PENFRO) ⬤⬤

The view of this historic town situated on a narrow ridge in the otherwise fairly flat landscape is dominated by the impressive ruins of **Pembroke Castle**. There are also some well preserved remains of the 14th-century town walls, including Barnard's Tower at the eastern end. For a long time, Pembroke was the regional centre (it also lent its name to a county, which has now been reinstated), but there was no real industrial growth; its port lost importance and business went elsewhere. Now the town mostly depends on tourists, who come to see the fortress with its massive cylindrical keep (23m high) and displays illustrating the history of the castle. Also popular are the Museum of the Home opposite the castle, with its thematic collection of everyday objects, and the two remaining medieval churches in the town with another in nearby Monkton.

ST DAVID'S (TYDDEWI) ✪✪✪

The provincial nature of this remarkably small cathedral city is undoubtedly due to its isolated location on the southwest corner of Wales. As well as the magnificent St David's Cathedral (▶ 22) you will find excellent beaches and coastal walks along the varied cliffs of the peninsula. The cathedral, the ruined medieval **Bishop's Palace** and the coastal path between St Justinian and Caerfai Bay (10.5km/6.5 miles) are the most important attractions of the city; there are other popular sights, such as the Oceanarium and St David's Farm Park, but these do not in themselves justify a long journey.

The neighbouring town of Solva is a small picturesque harbour on a long creek, which attracts many water-sports enthusiasts and tourists.

The bird reserve on Ramsey Island has limited access and can be reached by boat from St Justinian.

SKOMER, SKOKHOLM AND GRASSHOLM ✪✪✪

These three islands off the coast are a true paradise for nature lovers, and for birdwatchers in particular.

There are short daily crossings from Martin's Haven near Marloes to Skomer Island (except Mondays) at 10AM, 11AM or 12AM. This 292ha nature reserve is open to visitors (entrance fee) from Easter to the end of September or October (depending on the weather). There are prehistoric remains (including hut circles), butterflies, wild plants, various bird species, and seals.

The neighbouring Skokholm (97ha), which is also a breeding place for thousands of birds, including the Manx shearwater, can be visited only on Mondays between mid-June and a flexible date in September, provided that the one return service (10AM) from Martin's Haven is operating.

Mooring is not allowed at Grassholm, 16km (10 miles) off the coast. The nature reserve has some 30,000 gannets. Boat trips around the island are organised on Mondays (except on Bank Holidays) and Fridays at 10AM. For further information and reservations, contact the boat company Dale Sailing on 01646 601636.

 28A2

Bishop's Palace
☎ 01437 720517
🕐 Daily 9:30 (Sun 12) to 16, 17 or 18, depending on the season
♿ Reasonable
💷 Cheap

Above: *St David's Cathedral is sheltered in the Alun Valley*

✚ 28A1

✚ 28A1

Tudor Merchant's House
✉ Quay Hill
☎ 01834 842279
🕐 Apr–Sep, daily 10–5
   except Wed, Sun 1–5;
   Oct 10–3 except Wed,
   Sat, Sun 12–3
👢 Cheap

TENBY (DINBYCH-Y-PYSGOD)   ✪✪✪

A lively and, as far as the historic centre is concerned, picturesque seaside town, which despite its popularity has not been spoiled by mass tourism and has managed to retain much of its authentic, unaffected character. The compact old town, partly surrounded by medieval walls, contains narrow, atmospheric alleyways. The beautiful St Mary's Church, built between the 13th and 15th centuries in a combination of the Early English and Perpendicular styles, towers above the town – which was once a thriving port. There are two excellent beaches, North Beach and

South Beach. These are separated by Castle Hill, which offers good views. The slight remains of the 13th-century fortress are now partly used to house a local museum.

Just north of Castle Hill lies the sheltered, photogenic harbour closed off from the sea by a pier. To the south is St Catherine's Island with a Victorian fort, which was completed in 1875.

The South (or Five Arches) Gate is the only surviving entrance of the four original medieval gateways. Dating from the late 15th-century,

The seaside town of Tenby also has a beautiful harbour

the **Tudor Merchant's House** is a former merchant's dwelling that has been made into a museum; it is furnished to depict life from Tudor times onwards. The equally old Plantagenet House now serves as a pub. Near the harbour is the small St Julian's Chapel, a place of worship for fishermen dating from 1878.

Most forms of popular entertainment are outside the centre or in the surrounding area, including the Oakwood Leisure Park (16km/10 miles northwest via the A4075), and the Manor House zoo (5km/3 miles west on the B4318).

Caldey Island, with its interesting flora and wildlife, is suitable for a day trip. Boats from Tenby Harbour Pier provide a regular service to the island, which has been inhabited since prehistoric times. The abbey, founded by Cistercian monks in the 12th century, was dissolved in 1534 by order of Henry VIII. At the beginning of the 20th century the present monastery in Italian style was built for Anglican monks. The residents are now Cistercian monks from Belgium, who arrived in 1929 and make a living by selling home-made perfume and dairy products. Access to the monastery itself is restricted to men only.

A Walk along the Pembrokeshire Coast

This walk is an introduction to a characteristic section of the Pembrokeshire Coast, between Broad Haven and the Green Bridge. The route crosses parts reserved for military training, which occurs only at certain times and places. Broad Haven is a secluded bay surrounded by cliffs and has a beautiful sandy beach.

Following the coast path in a southwesterly direction, you pass St Govan's Head with a coast guard lookout on the top. Not long afterwards, you reach St Govan's Chapel. Further west, Huntsman's Leap comes into view, the first of a number of ravines.

The curious, 13th century chapel, originally a 6th-century hermit's cell, is hidden between steep cliffs. The natural spring that belongs to it has dried up. The somewhat obscure St Govan was possibly Gawaine, knight of King Arthur's Round Table. According to legend, a hunter who jumped over the ravine on horseback and looked back had such a fright that he had a heart attack.

The path continues, high above the sea, through an open landscape. Suddenly, a number of curious rock formations come into view.

The two chalk Elegug Stacks (Stack Rocks), which rise like pillars from the sea, are a popular breeding place for waterbirds. The Green Bridge of Wales, a naturally formed arch, is one of the most photogenic shapes along this part of the coast.

Return via the same route, with the option of turning inland to Bosherston at St Govan's Chapel.

Distance
13km (8 miles) there and back

Time
4 hours

Start/end point
Bosherston or Broad Haven car parks
✚ 28A1
From the Bosherston car park walk through the idyllic Lily Ponds to the start point at Broad Haven.

Lunch
Pub in Bosherston

The Green Bridge of Wales on the Pembrokeshire coast

South Wales

In the 18th and 19th centuries the discovery of coal and iron ore made south Wales into the most industrialised and most urbanised part of the principality. It still is, although the mines, wharfs and factories have long been replaced by high-tech industries.

In between the factory complexes and residential terraces there are many beautiful things to see: the remarkably large number of country parks and, of course, a wealth of industrial archaeology. The Gower peninsula is, rightly, a protected area, and Wales's two largest cities, Cardiff and Swansea, have excellent museums, good shops and a wide range of entertainments.

This region is also where you will encounter two typically Welsh phenomena: rugby and male-voice choirs.

> *'The ancient land of my fathers*
> *is dear to me,*
> *A land of poets and minstrels,*
> *famed men.*
> *Her brave warriors, patriots*
> *much blessed,*
> *It was for freedom that they lost*
> *their blood.'*

Part of the Welsh national anthem

Left: *the Gower coast near Rhossili and Worms Head*

Cardiff (Caerdydd)

Cardiff (325,000 inhabitants) is the capital of Wales and fulfils this role with verve as well as visible status. Despite a history that goes back as the Romans, this is a relatively young city. Its real growth did not begin until the 19th century under the impassioned patronage of the marquesses of Bute, who owned large parts of the area. The number of inhabitants rose from 1000 in 1800 to 170,000 in 1900; this trend is set to continue. Since its election in 1955 as the official capital, the city is going through a second period of prosperity. The renovation of the harbour quarter around Cardiff Bay is, for the time being, the highlight of this development.

In exploring Cardiff, there are three parts that each represent the most important periods in the city's history. The first part is the historic centre with Cardiff Castle, the place where it all began in about AD 60.

North of this is Cathays Park, with the early 20th-century Civic Centre, an area where the city clearly demonstrates that it is the cultural, educational, legal and administrative centre of the principality.

And in the south is Cardiff Bay, which shows the Welsh in progressive mood, without relying on their reputation and heritage.

Cardiff City Hall is a fine example of grand Edwardian architecture

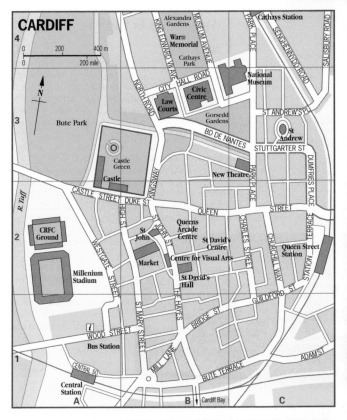

CARDIFF

4

0   200   400 m
0   200 mile

N

Alexandra Gardens
War Memorial
Cathays Park
Cathays Station
MUSEUM AVENUE
PARK PLACE
SENGHENNYDD ROAD
SALISBURY ROAD
KINGS LEONARD WAY
CITY HALL ROAD
NORTH ROAD
National Museum
Civic Centre
Law Courts
Gorsedd Gardens
ST ANDREW'S PL
St Andrew
BD DE NANTES
STUTTGARTER ST
Bute Park
3
Castle Green
Castle
KINGSWAY
New Theatre
PARK PLACE
DUMFRIES PLACE
CASTLE STREET   DUKE ST
HIGH ST
QUEEN   STREET
R. Taff
CRFC Ground
WESTGATE STREET
St John
Queens Arcade Centre
St David's Centre
CHARLES STREET
CHURCHILL WAY
STATION TERRACE
Queen Street Station
2
Market
Centre for Visual Arts
St David's Hall
Millenium Stadium
ST MARY STREET
THE HAYES
BRIDGE ST
GUILDEORD ST
WOOD STREET
i
Bus Station
MILL LANE
BUTE TERRACE
ADAMS T
1
CENTRAL SQ
Central Station
BUTE TERRACE
A   **B** ↑ Cardiff Bay   **C**

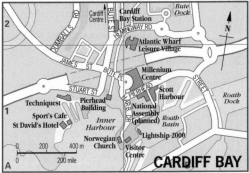

CARDIFF BAY

2

Cardiff Centre
Bute Dock
Cardiff Bay Station
HEMINGWAY RD
DUMBALLS RD
BUTE ST
Atlantic Wharf Leisure Village
JAMES ST
BUTE PL
Millenium Centre
STUART ST
Scott Harbour
PIERHEAD
Techniquest
Pierhead Building
HARBOUR DR
National Assembly (planned)
Roath Dock
Sport's Cafe
St David's Hotel
Inner Harbour
Roath Basin
Lightship 2000
Norwegian Church
Visitor Centre

N

Roath Dock

0   200   400 m
0   200 mile

1

A

What to See in Cardiff

Techniquest

- 73A1 (bottom map)
- Stuart Street
- 029 20475475
- Mon–Fri 9:30–4:30, Sat–Sun 10:30–5
- Café
- Very good
- Reasonable

The Queen's Arcade shopping centre in Cardiff

CARDIFF BAY   ●●

The harbour and former Tiger Bay area is currently undergoing extensive restoration work. The Cardiff Bay Barrage (costing £191 million) was built first, creating an immense freshwater lake; the Inner Harbour was then tackled. Much was demolished, but here and there remarkable buildings remain, such as the Victorian Pierhead Building (1896) and the white Norwegian Church (1868), intended for seamen but now used as an arts centre. A number of new buildings are finished, some with very modern features, such as the small, tubular Visitor Centre and the huge St David's Hotel. Mermaid Quay houses many shops, cafés and restaurants, and Crafts in the Bay (on the corner of Bute Street and Bute Place) shows Welsh arts and crafts. The Wales Millennium Centre will become the home of the Welsh National Opera. The Welsh Assembly, too, will eventually have a new, if controversial, building created by the architect Richard Rogers. The museums in the Bay include the Welsh Industrial Maritime Museum and **Techniquest**. The latter is great fun for young people. It gives a practical, hands-on experience of the many aspects of science and technology and includes a planetarium.

- 73A3 (top map)
- Castle Street
- 029 20878100
- Mar–Oct, 9:30–6; Nov–Feb, 9:30–4:30
- Tearoom
- Only the grounds are accessible
- Moderate

CARDIFF CASTLE AND TOWN CENTRE   ●●

In about AD 60 the Romans built a fortification on this spot. In 1081 the Normans established a wooden castle on the site, which in the 12th century was replaced by the stone keep, which is still standing. Nevertheless, it is the 19th-century renovations and extensions that are of especial interest. These were carried out by the architect and designer William Burgess for the immeasurably rich third marquess of Bute. Extravagant and dazzling (others may say: bizarre) are descriptions that are eminently applicable to the state rooms and added structures, such as the clock tower. It is a curious, extremely Victorian combination of Gothic, neoclassical, Pre-Raphaelite and even Arabic styles, with themes such as the Bible, Chaucer's *Canterbury Tales*, Greek mythology and the Scottish countryside.

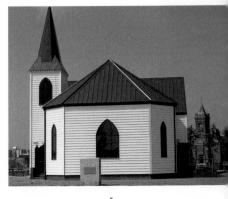

The reasonably well-planned city centre of Cardiff is a fascinating combination of old and new. Historic sights include the late Gothic St John's Church with its slender 15th-century tower; the adjacent indoor market dating from 1891; the New Theatre from 1906; and the covered Victorian and Edwardian shopping galleries.

The wooden Norwegian Church now serves as an arts centre

Contemporary places of interest include indoor shopping centres such as the St David's Centre, the Queen's Arcade and the Capitol Centre, the St David's Concert Hall (seats 2,000) and the International Arena (seats 5,500). The impressive Millennium Stadium (replacing the demolished Cardiff Arms Park) seats 72,000 and is the home of Welsh rugby and one of the most modern stadiums in Europe.

CASTELL COCH ✪✪

The extraordinary Castell Coch is a creation by William Burges for the third marquess of Bute. From the outside, this fortress surrounded by woods seems to have come straight out of a fairy story, but on the inside it shows the same curious Victorian opulence as Cardiff Castle. It was intended as a country retreat, but was hardly ever used. However, the Bute children were sometimes brought here if there was danger of infection in the city.

✚ 29C1
✉ North of Cardiff. Junction 32 of the M4, then the A470 to Tongwynlais
☎ 029 20810101
🕐 Apr–May, Oct, daily 9:30–5; Jun–Sep, daily 9:30–6; Nov–Mar, Mon–Sat 9:30–4, Sun 11–4
🍴 Tearoom 🖐 Cheap

CATHAYS PARK ✪✪

On the northern edge of the city centre lies the spacious Cathays Park, which is mainly taken up by the Civic Centre, built in white Portland stone in the neoclassical Edwardian style.

National Museum of Wales
✚ 73C3 (top map)
✉ Cathays Park
☎ 029 20397951
🕐 Tue–Sun 10–5
🍴 Restaurant
♿ Very good
🖐 Moderate. Children free

> ### DID YOU KNOW?
>
> During a walk through the Welsh capital, the marquesses of Bute will crop up many times. This Scottish family arrived in Cardiff in 1766. The second marquess acquired his substantial riches from coal, and in 1839 built the first dock. The third marquess (1847-1900) was one of the wealthiest men in the world. After World War II, the Butes returned to the Scottish island of the same name.

The most prominent place is occupied by the City Hall (1901–5), of which the most interesting parts are the council chamber and the marble hall with its statues of the 'heroes of Wales' (► 72). To the left of the City Hall stand the Law Courts (1906), and to the right the **National Museum of Wales** (1912–27). The collection of French Impressionists and the Evolution of Wales exhibition are especially worthwhile.

The Welsh National War Memorial (1928) stands slightly further north and is surrounded by university buildings and several government institutions.

DYFFRYN GARDENS ✪✪

These formal 28ha gardens are among the most beautiful in Wales. They are part of the landscape park surrounding the neo-classical Dyffryn House (1893), which belonged to the Cory family. The house is now a conference centre, but the gardens have remained virtually unchanged during their hundred years of existence.

LLANDAFF CATHEDRAL ✪✪

The restored, medieval Llandaff Cathedral is surprisingly set in village surroundings. The nave is dominated by Jacob Epstein's sculpture *Christ in Majesty*.

The open-air **Museum of Welsh Life** contains more than 30 authentic Welsh buildings, including a chapel, school, and traditional farms and cottages. Craftsmen demonstrate their trades, and St Fagan's Castle dating from about 1580 boasts a 19th-century interior and lovely formal gardens.

Below: Dyffryn Gardens are certainly worth a visit

🕀 29C1
✉ Via the A48 from junction 33 of the M4
☎ 029 20593328
🕐 Daily 10–sunset
🍴 Tearoom 👍 Very good
💷 Cheap. Free in winter

🕀 29C1
Museum of Welsh Life
✉ St Fagans
🚌 From the city centre
☎ 029 20573500
🕐 Tue–Sun from 10
🍴 Restaurant
👍 Very good.
💷 Moderate. Children free

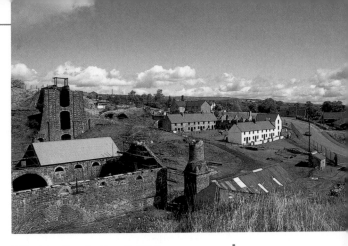

What to See in South Wales

BLAENAVON ⚫⚫

In 1757 this industrial town saw the founding of the Blaenavon **Ironworks**, which grew into one of the largest and most advanced in the country. There are substantial remains of blast furnaces and workers' cottages from 1789–92, part of an industrial landscape that is now a World Heritage Site. The production process is clearly shown.

The **Big Pit Mining Museum** is a tourist attraction created by former miners. It was opened in 1983, some years after the coal mine had permanently closed. Above ground there is much to see, but it is the tour underground that stirs the imagination. A lift-cage takes visitors down to the shafts, which are situated at a depth of 90m. Just north of Blaenavon is the beautiful Clydach Gorge.

CAERLEON (CAERLLION) ⚫⚫

Isca fort, which the Romans built here in about AD 75, served as a base for the 6,000-strong Augustan Second Legion. With an area of some 20ha it was one of the largest fortifications in Europe. Excavations in the 20th century exposed a number of impressive buildings: a 1st-century amphitheatre that could seat the entire legion; 64 barracks arranged side by side; and the **Fortress Baths**, a huge bathhouse complex. The more important discoveries are displayed in the Legionary Museum.

CAERPHILLY (CAERFFILI) CASTLE ⚫⚫⚫

All kinds of superlatives apply to this moated, late-13th century fortress. It is certainly one of the most impressive, largest and best-preserved castles in Britain, and it is also one of the most successful examples of a concentric walls-within-walls design. It gives an impression of being impregnable, which is perhaps confirmed by the fact that the castle was never captured. The leaning southeast tower is almost as dramatic as the more famous structure at Pisa.

➕ 29C1

Ironworks and Big Pit Mining Museum

✉ In the northeastern valleys, on the A4043

☎ Ironworks 01495 792615; Big Pit 01495 790311

🕐 Ironworks Easter–Sep, 10–4; Big Pit Mar–Nov, 9:30–5. Last underground tour 3:30

🚌 23 or 30 from Pontypool

♿ Neither suitable

💷 Ironworks cheap; Big Pit moderate

➕ 29D1

Caerleon Fortress Baths

🚌 60 from Newport or Monmouth

♿ Very good 💷 Cheap

Above: *the industrial archaeology of Blaenavon Ironworks*

➕ 29C1

✉ On the edge of the town

☎ 01222 883143

🕐 9:30–4, 5 or 6, depending on the season

🚉 Caerphilly

🚌 70 and 71 from Cardiff

♿ Good, except higher parts

💷 Cheap

77

28B1

Gower Heritage Centre
✉ Parkmill
☎ 01792 371206
🕐 Daily 10–4:30 or 5:30, depending on the season
Moderate
Good

Oxwich Castle
☎ 01792 390359
🕐 May–Sep, 10–5
Cheap
Good

GOWER (GWYR) ✪✪✪

A beautiful green peninsula beyond Swansea, Gower is an Area of Outstanding Natural Beauty measuring some 29km by 12km. Despite its relatively small size, Gower has a varied landscape. Inland it consists of undulating fields and arable land, alternating with long stretches of moorland, woods and narrow valleys. In the north, Gower is bordered by endless tidal marshes and mudflats, such as the flat Llanrhidian Marsh, part of the wide estuary of the Loughor.

The west coast is largely taken up by the sandy beach of the 6km-wide Rhossili Bay, protected by high rock faces and cliffs of Burry Holms and the photogenic, windy promontory called Worms Head (▶ 79).

In contrast, the south coast is an attractive series of cliffs, secluded bays, spacious beaches and cosy villages. This is most visited part and is also the most anglicised.

Gower is ideal for an active holiday. There is swimming, sunbathing and windsurfing on the popular beaches at the Mumbles, Langland, Limeslade and Caswell (all with facilities); in the beautiful but less easily accessible Brandy Cove, Pwlldu Bay and Threecliffs Bay; and near striking places such as Oxwich with its dunes, and Port Eynon, which used to be a notorious smugglers' nest; or in the very wide but practically deserted Rhossili Bay. Gower also provides great opportunities for walking, cycling and horse riding.

There are prehistoric remains (Parc le Breos near **Parkmill**, Arthur's Stone, both neolithic chamber tombs) and evocative castle ruins (Oystermouth, Weobley, **Oxwich**). Among the rural villages inland is Reynoldston, with a pub and a village green. Closer to Swansea are lively seaside towns, such as the Mumbles with a pier. There is a love spoon gallery just along the coast in Oystermouth.

Rhossili Bay on the west coast of Gower

DID YOU KNOW?

The wooden love spoon is part of Welsh folklore and is one of the best-known craft items in the country. A potential lover would give a home-made spoon to the girl he wanted to court – a tradition dating from the early 17th century. If the love spoon was accepted, this meant that the girl agreed to marriage. Because of the enormous variety of symbols (keys, anchors, hearts, flowers, necklaces), no two love spoons are the same.

A Walk to Worms Head

The most impressive landscape on the Gower peninsula is found near Rhossili (Rholsili) and Worms Head, which is sometimes called the 'Land's End of Gower'. The area is a combination of rugged cliffs and sandy bays, divided by the windy headland of Worms Head.

Walk from the Rhosilli car park to the coastguard station on the western point of the headland.

En route you will see, on your right, Rhossili Bay – 6km (4 miles) of sandy beach – which is 400m wide at low tide. It is backed by the sandstone Rhossili Down, at 193m the highest point in Gower.

Steps lead down to the causeway, which floods at high tide. A tide timetable is available from the visitor centre at the starting point. The causeway is accessible for two-and-a-half hours before and after low tide.

Worms Head consists of two islets, Inner and outer Head, linked by the rocky path of Devil's Bridge. The outer islet is a bird reserve with sea coots, fulmars, kittiwakes, razorbills and cormorants. The name Worms Head derives from the Scandinavian *orme*, meaning snake, perhaps named because this string of rocks looks rather like a snake or dragon.

You can return by the same path, or you can explore the coast a little further, for example by turning right (with your back to Worms Head) and following the cliffs up to the remote Fall and Mewslade bays, which merge into each other. You have now reached one of the most isolated parts of Gower.

Distance
6km (4 miles), including Worms Head and Mewslade Bay

Time
2 hours

Start/end point
Car park at Worms Head Visitor Centre
➕ 28B1

Lunch
Worms Head Hotel

The narrow headland of Worms Head

28B1

Glynn Vivian Art Gallery
✉ Alexandra Road
☎ 01792 655006
🕐 Tue–Sun, bank holidays
   10–5
♿ Ground floor only
🎫 Free

Maritime and Industrial Museum
✉ Maritime Quarter
☎ 01792 650351
🕐 Tue–Sun, bank holidays
   10–5
🍴 Café (only in summer)
♿ Very good
🎫 Free

Phantasia
✉ Parc Tawe, North Dock
☎ 01792 474555
🕐 Tue–Sun 10–5. Open
   bank holidays and
   Mondays in high season
🎫 Cheap

Swansea, the Dylan Thomas Theatre

SWANSEA (ABERTAWE) ★

Wales's second city suffered extensive damage during World War II. Yet amid the modern rebuilding there survive odd corners of the old town, especially around the ruins of the medieval castle. Its best-known inhabitant, the poet Dylan Thomas (► 14), spoke of 'this ugly, beautiful city'.

For the visitor Swansea provides a wide range of facilities for entertainment and outings. There are several partially covered shopping centres, including the traditional Swansea Market Hall, where fresh produce is sold, including local cockles. Further, there are various theatres and concert halls, and excellent sporting facilities, such as the large leisure centre with its famous swimming oasis and a marina for more than 600 boats.

There are also plenty of museums. The Swansea Museum (Victoria Road), featuring the city and its region, dates from 1838 and is the oldest in Wales. The **Glynn Vivian Art Gallery** specialises in paintings, porcelain and ceramics, while the **Maritime and Industrial Museum** explores the history of Swansea as a port and industrial city. The university's Taliesin Arts Centre houses a remarkable collection of Egyptology, and Ty Lien (Somerset Place) is the National Literature Centre of Wales, a remnant of the Year of Literature (1995).

Phantasia consists of tropical greenhouses with some 5,000 plants, an aquarium, aviary, reptile collection and butterfly house. The Clyne Gardens with their azaleas and rhododendrons are most beautiful in May, and the leafy Singleton Park has a botanical garden as well as a boating lake.

THE VALLEYS ⊙⊙

Between the Brecon Beacons National Park and the M4 lie the populous, heavily industrialised 'Valleys'. They run almost without exception from north to south. The most interesting ones are briefly discussed below. The order is from west (Vale of Neath) to east (Blaenavon–Cwmbran–Newport).

The Vale of Neath and the adjacent Dulais Valley north of the industrial town of Neath (Castell-Nedd), home to the 'Welsh All Blacks' (Neath Rugby Club), are known for a number of tourist attractions. The extensive ruins of Neath Abbey, founded in 1130, provide a peaceful haven in the urban surroundings, though the gloomy industrial estate nearby makes it difficult to imagine the Middle Ages. The Aberdulais Falls is a beautiful waterfall in a narrow, green ravine, painted by Turner and other landscape artists; it also boasts the largest waterwheel in Europe. There is an interpretive centre at the site. In Crynant, along the Dulais Valley, you can visit the **Cefn Coed Colliery Museum** at one of the last coal mines in Wales (closed in 1990). Visitors can still experience how a mine was run.

The Afan Valley (Cwm Afan) runs eastwards from Port Talbot (A4107). A large part of the slopes was planted with conifers by the Forestry Commission prior to World War II, which has given the valley its nickname 'Little Switzerland'. The huge Afan Argoed Forest Park is an ideal place for walking or cycling (bicycle hire on site). The South Wales Miners' Museum in the park gives an impression of the life of a miner and is part of a countryside centre near Cynonville.

✚ 29C/D1

Cefn Coed Colliery Museum
- ✉ Crynant, via the A4109
- ☎ 01639 750556
- ⊕ Apr–Oct, 10:30–5
- 🚌 158 from Swansea or Neath
- ♿ Very good

Above: *a waterfall in the Vale of Neath*

There are two Rhondda valleys: Rhondda Fach (small) and Rhondda Fawr (large). These are typical of the south-eastern valleys. They are small and steep, which is why the houses (as in Treorchy and Treherbert) had to be built in long terraces. None of the dozens of mines offering work to some 150,000 labourers in the 19th century is still in use, and the valleys have been considerably cleared up since then. A special Rhondda Heritage Trail leads past the most interesting points (leaflet available from local tourist office). The highlight for many visitors is the **Rhondda Heritage Park** in the grounds of the Lewis-Merthyr mine in Trehafod, which closed in 1983. An underground guided tour is part of the visit. The route from the northern end of the Rhondda (Hirwaun) is also worth a mention; the A4061 is one of the most beautiful sections of road in the region.

Aberdare lies at the northern end of the fairly open and wide Cynon Valley. The 194ha Dare Valley Country Park, with its lakes, forests and moorland, offers plenty of opportunities to explore this delightful area and there are several activities on offer. Information is available at the visitor centre.

The most important place in the Taff valley is Merthyr Tydfil, the former iron-production capital of Wales. The 19th-century **Cyfarthfa Castle**, surrounded by a park, was once the home of the powerful ironmaster William Crawshay. It is now a museum and art gallery focusing on the industrial and social past of the town and its surrounding area. The mansion is in sharp contrast with the simple ironworkers' cottages in Chapel Row. The composer **Joseph Parry** lived at No. 4; his work is still included in the repertoire of many male-voice choirs.

There are many other reminders of Merthyr's past as an important industrial centre, but this modernised town is now looking to the future. For example, as a stopoff for the Brecon Beacons, of which a part (the lovely lake area around Pontsticill) can be explored by means of the Brecon Mountain Railway.

Rhondda Heritage Park

- ✉ Trehafod near Pontypridd
- ☎ 01443 682036
- ⏰ Daily 10–6. Closed Mondays in winter
- 🍴 Restaurant
- Trehafod
- ♿ Very good
- Moderate

The River Taff near Pontypridd

Cyfarthfa Castle Museum

- ☎ 01685 723112
- ⏰ Apr–Sep, daily 10–5:30; Oct–Mar, Mon–Fri 10–4, Sat–Sun 12–4
- 🍴 Tearoom
- Merthyr Tydfil
- ♿ Very good   Cheap

Joseph Parry's Cottage

- ☎ 01685 723112
- ⏰ Easter–Sep, Thu–Sun 14–5
- Merthyr Tydfil
- ♿ Very good   Cheap

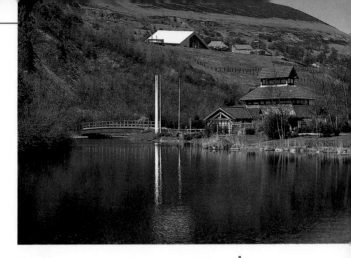

Above: *Victoria Park in Ebbw Vale town*

Sights in the Rhymney Valley include Bute Town (Drenewydd, north of Rhymney) built in 1803 according to a set plan; the Drenewydd Museum there gives a good impression of the living conditions of Welsh ironworkers. Parc Bryn Bach (near Tredegar) is a successful attempt to give a deserted industrial area a new lease of life as a country park. The same applies to Parc Cwm Darran (4km south of Rhymney), which is suitable for walking, cycling and angling. The large and imposing Caerphilly Castle lies at the southern end of the Rhymney Valley (▶ 77). Leading across the tops of the slopes is the 43km (27-mile) Rhymney Valley Ridgeway Walk, which offers beautiful views across the valleys.

The Sirhowy Valley can also be explored on foot – a long-distance path of the same name extends for 41km (26 miles). Just south of Blackwood you can visit the 16th-century Gelligroes watermill. The Sirhowy Valley Country Park at Crosskeys is not only one of the most attractive, but at 405ha is also one of the largest in south Wales.

Crosskeys also has a link with the Cwmcarn Forest Drive in the Ebbw Vale, an 11km (7-mile) route for cars through the Ebbw Forest with splendid views and plenty of opportunities for picnicking and walking on the way. There is a visitor centre at the entrance.

The Ironworks and the Big Pit Mining Museum in Blaenavon (▶ 77) are two excellent reminders of the industrial history of this region, as is the **Valley Heritage Museum** in Pontypool. It is housed in the stables of Park House, which once belonged to the Hanbury family of ironmasters. The Llandegfedd Reservoir is popular with water-sports enthusiasts, and Cwmbran is a new town with excellent facilities for shopping, excursions and sports.

Finally, a sombre reminder of the human cost of mining is the memorial at Aberfan in the Taff Valley, where 116 children and 28 adults died when a slag heap collapsed on the local school.

Valley Heritage Museum

- ✉ Pontypool, Park House estate
- 🕐 Mon–Sat 10–5, Sun 2–5. Closed Christmas and New Year
- 🍴 Café
- 🚌 From Pontypool Town Hall
- ♿ Very good 💷 Cheap

The Borderlands

The border area of Wales shares many characteristics with its English neighbour. There are more small market towns, and Welsh is relatively little spoken here. You can also see the black-and-white timber-framing that is so typical of the traditional houses east of Offa's Dyke.

The northern border region offers great variety. The Clwydian Range is an Area of Outstanding Natural Beauty, and the small, densely forested Vale of Llangollen is equally attractive. Erddig, Chirk Castle and Powis Castle are three country houses of great appeal in this part of Wales.

The central border area is a landscape of rolling hills, as are the pastoral Black Mountains that form the eastern range of the Brecon Beacons. The southern borderland is dominated by the River Wye, which winds its way through wooded valleys past the ruins of castles and abbeys.

> *'What Wales lacks and has
> always needed most,
> Is not an eastern border
> but an eastern coast.'*

HARRI WEBB

———————•———————

Left: *the River Dee at Llangollen*

🚩 29C4

✉ 12km (7 miles) south of Wrexham (via A483)

☎ 01691 777701

🕐 Apr–Sep, Wed–Sun 12–5; Oct, Wed–Sun 12–4. Open on bank holidays. Gardens: 11–6 (5 in Oct)

🍴 Tearoom

🚌 2A Wrexham–Oswestry

🚉 Chirk, 0.5km from entrance, 2.5km (1½ miles) from castle

♿ Very good Moderate

🚩 29C5

Above: *wrought-iron baroque gates at Chirk Castle*

CHIRK CASTLE ✪✪✪

This border castle dates from the late 13th and early 14th centuries and owes its robust appearance to Edward I. In later centuries the interior underwent frequent changes, as the Myddleton family (owners since 1595) turned the fortress into a country house.

The rooms have skilful plasterwork and contain valuable paintings, Gobelin tapestries, and furniture in the Adam style. The surrounding 18th-century park is worthwhile by itself, especially for the stylish 19th-century yew topiary, beautiful trees, rare shrubs and wrought-iron gates by the Davies brothers, made in 1719.

CLWYDIAN RANGE ✪✪

This 35km (22-mile) hill ridge rises between the flat landscape of the Dee estuary (popular with visitors from the English Midlands) and the fertile Vale of Clwyd. Near the broad tops, the fields and woods of the lower slopes gradually give way to moorland covered with grass, heather or ferns. There are a number of prehistoric sites on the range.

Offa's Dyke Path (▶88) follows the watershed of the range along its entire length, passing peaks such as the Moel Llanfair (447m), Moel Famau (554m), Foel Fenlli (511m) and Moel Llys-y-coed (465m). The inhabitants of the small stone hamlets at the foot of the slopes are mainly farmers who make a living from hill farming (sheep) and dairy cattle.

LLANGOLLEN ✪✪

A friendly and lively border town, nestling in the narrow valley of the River Dee. The town put itself on the culture map in 1947 by organising the first **International Musical Eisteddfod**, which takes place annually in July. At this international festival of music and dance, which draws some 150,000 spectators, ethnic communities (as the Celtic Welsh are themselves) are given a platform to celebrate their own culture. This is partly why Llangollen is home to the European Centre for Traditional and Regional Cultures.

The town is popular with tourists. Attractions include a trip by steam train (13km/8 mile section) or pull boat; visiting a car, postal or school museum; and walking, angling and white-water canoeing on the river. The compact town centre has some buildings of interest, such as the bridge and the parish church (fine ceiling), both of medieval origin.

Plas Newydd (Butler Hill) is a black-and-white timber-framed country house, which was the home of two eccentric lady friends – the ladies of Llangollen – between 1780 and 1829. Both the interior and the surrounding garden are well worth a visit.

A path close to the quayside leads up to the steep hill above the town (275m) with beautiful views and the ruins of Castell Dinas Bran, built around 1260 by the lords of Powys. The romantic remains of **Valle Crucis Abbey** are more substantial and have a special beauty. The Cistercian abbey was founded in 1201 under the patronage of the welsh lord of northern Powys. The church shows the features of the Early English Gothic style, and the chapter house and parts of the dormitory are well preserved. Valle Crucis lies just south of the impressive Horseshoe Pass (417m), which leads to the Llantysilio Mountain range.

The Pontcysyllte Aqueduct from 1805 is an example of the skill of the engineer Thomas Telford (follow the A5 for 7km/4 miles east towards Chirk). At a height of 36m, the Shropshire Union Canal is channelled across the River Dee via a channel measuring 300m in length and 3m in width. It is possible to cross by (motor) boat or on foot .

✚ 29C4

Plas Newydd
- ✉ Hill Street
- ☎ 01978 861314
- ◷ Apr–Oct, daily 10–5
- ♿ Very good
- 💷 Cheap

Valle Crucis Abbey
- ✉ 3.5km (2 miles) west on the A542; follow the road to Ruthin/Denbigh
- ☎ 01978 860326
- ◷ May–Sep, daily 10–5
- ♿ Good
- 💷 Cheap

International Musical Eisteddfod
- ✉ Royal International Pavilion, Abbey Road LL20 8SW
- ☎ 01978 860236, fax 01978 861300, e-mail info@lime.uk.com, www.international-eisteddfod.co.uk

Valle Crucis Abbey

Not marked on the map

Offa's Dyke Association, West Street, Knighton, Powys LD7 1EN

☎ 01547 528753,
www.offa.demon.co.uk/
offa.htm

OFFA'S DYKE ⭐⭐

In the late 8th century King Offa of Mercia (central England) built a 129km (80-mile) earthen rampart and ditch along the border with Wales. It runs from Chepstow northwards to Prestatyn and incorporates natural features for some sections. Its main aim was a clear demarcation of his own territory, since the dyke was limited as a line of defence – it was too weak and there was no standing garrison to hold off any attackers. Offa's Dyke is well preserved in several places, including near Knighton (Tref-y-Clawwd), which also has an information centre (West Street). Elsewhere it has disappeared or is only a few metres high.

The 288km (179-mile) Offa's Dyke Path (➤ 86), a designated national trail, follows the dyke across a 112km (70-mile) stretch.

29D2

White Castle

✉ Minor roads from B4233 at Llantilio Crossenny

☎ 01600 780380

🕐 May–Sep, 10–5

💰 Cheap

THE THREE CASTLES ⭐

In the Monnow Valley, a remote corner of southeast Wales, stand the attractive ruins of three fairly small medieval fortresses at a distance of 8–11km (5–7 miles) from each other. The Normans originally built these castles (initially of wood) in the exposed and restless borderland between the Wye Valley and the Black Mountains.

The mighty keep of Skenfrith Castle

White Castle, Skenfrith and Grosmont can all be visited, but if time is short visit just the first-mentioned, which probably speaks most to the imagination.

The Three Castles Walk is a 29km (18-mile) route, which includes all three castle (➤ 114).

VALE OF EWYAS (➤ 26, TOP TEN)

WELSHPOOL (Y TRALLWNG) ✪✪

This market town is little different from similar places on the English side of the border. The wide high street is lined by buildings that greatly vary in size, style and age. The atmosphere is friendly and lively, especially on Monday, the traditional market day.

You can make a boat trip on the restored Montgomery Canal and a former warehouse on the quayside is now a regional museum and centre. The impressive 19th-century railway station has been transformed into a shopping centre. It is, however, still possible in Welshpool to take the train: conventional trains run here as well as the Welshpool and Llanfair Railway, a 13km (8-mile) steam-train section to Llanfair Caereinion.

The main attraction in Welshpool is **Powis Castle**, founded by Welsh princes around 1200, and later inhabited by the Herberts (marquesses and earls of Powis). The splendid interior with its valuable paintings, tapestries and furniture, the truly magnificent terraced gardens in Italian and French style, and the associations with Robert Clive, better known as Clive of India (1725–74), make this stately home one of the most exquisite in Wales.

South of Welshpool is the former county town of Montgomery. This particularly charming place has a mixture of buildings, predominantly in the Georgian style. The 13th-century church has a beautiful choir screen and ceiling, and interesting memorials. The ruins of the castle built in 1233 and dismantled in 1649 are especially pleasing because of their fine location on a narrow ridge, which offers beautiful views. There are a number of pleasant inns in the town.

WYE VALLEY (▶ 24, TOP TEN)

✚ 29C3

Powis Castle

⊠ On the southwestern edge of Welshpool

☎ 01938 554338

🕐 Apr–Oct, Wed–Sun 1–5; Jul–Aug, Tue–Sun 1–5. Open bank holidays. Garden: 11–6

🍴 Tearoom

Ⓟ Welshpool; 3km (2-mile) walk

♿ Very limited access to house and garden

💷 Fairly expensive (but value for money)

Above: *the main street in Welshpool*
Below: *ornamental stonework on the garden terraces at Powis Castle*

A Walk through the Wye Valley

Distance
12km (7.5 miles)

Time
3 hours

Start point
Chepstow Castle
✚ 29D1

End point
Brockweir
✚ Not marked on the map

Lunch, coffee or tea breaks
At Tintern Abbey, The Old Station (Tintern) or pub in Brockweir

Inside the keep of Chepstow Castle

This route follows the first 12km (7.5 miles) of the 230km (144-mile) Wye Valley Walk from Chepstow to Rhayader. This section has three highlights: Chepstow Castle, Eagle's Nest and Tintern Abbey (▶ 24). The reasonably good bus service between Chepstow (Cas-Gwent) and Monmouth (the No. 69, every two hours from Monday to Saturday) makes it possible to return to the starting point by public transport. The Wye Valley was popular as a tourist attraction as early as the 19th century, as is evident from the words of William Wordsworth in1798:

'Five years have past; five summers with the length
Of long winters! and again I hear
These waters, rolling from their mountain-springs
With a soft inland murmur. —Once again
Do I behold these steep and lofty cliffs,
That on a wild secluded scene impress
Thoughts of more deep seclusion; and connect
The landscape with the quiet of the sky.'
From: *Lines Composed A Few Miles Above Tintern Abbey*

The starting point is the car park at Chepstow Castle. Follow the Walk signs. The first part up to Wynd Cliff leads through lovely woods, which here and there make way for panoramas across the Wye Valley.

At Wynd Cliff you can make a short detour to Eagle's Nest, built in 1828 as a tourist attraction; 365 steps lead up to the 215m-high viewpoint.

The path now passes Minepit Wood, where beeches have been planted to cover the traces of former iron ore mines. In spring the ground is covered in bluebells. An old packhorse route then leads to Tintern.

The ruined abbey is one of the most beautiful (for its location as well as architecture) in Britain. There are several points for stopping – one of them at the former railway station (1.5 km/1 mile further on), now used as an information centre and a place for refreshments.

The last section leads from the old station along the western shore to pleasant, unpretentious Brockweir, which lies on the opposite, English side of the river (there is a bridge).

Where To...

Top: *antiques in Monmouth*
Right: *the International Musical Eisteddfod in Llangollen*

Northwest Wales

Vegetarian Dishes
Generally, vegetarians are well catered for in Wales. Most pubs and inns have one or more meatless dishes on the menu, and the same applies to the slightly more upmarket restaurants. The *Vegetarian Visitor* brochure is available from the British Tourist Office, and includes more than 300 addresses.

Aberdaron, Lleyn Peninsula
Y Gegin Fawr (£)
Simple restaurant in 14th-century stopping-place for pilgrims. Small terrace. Suitable for lunch or tea.
✉ **In the centre near the bridge**

Abersoch, Lleyn Peninsula
Riverside (££)
Popular hotel and restaurant. The cuisine has an excellent reputation. Beautiful garden along the river.
✉ **On the A499**
☎ **01758 712419**

Beaumaris, Anglesey
Ye Olde Bulls Head (££–£££)
Five-hundred-year-old inn within walking distance of the famous castle. One of the best addresses in North Wales.
✉ **Castle Street**
☎ **01248 810329**

Betws-y-coed
Ty Gwyn (£–££)
Cosy, old-fashioned inn, with good food. Game and fish, as well as vegetarian dishes.
✉ **On the A5, near Waterloo Bridge, 750m from the centre**
☎ **01690 710383**

Bodfari
Dinorben Arms (£)
Atmospheric 17th-century pub with beautiful view. A good place to stop for food or drink during a trip across the Clwydian Range. Local dishes made with fresh ingredients.
✉ **On the A541, northeast of Denbigh. Follow signs for Tremeirchion from Bodfari**

Capel Curig
Bryn Tyrch Hotel (£)
Popular halfway house for walkers and climbers. Specialises in vegetarian dishes.
✉ **On the A5, not far from Betws-y-coed**

Conwy
The Old Rectory (£££)
Not cheap, but you get value for money in this elegant luxury country house hotel. Gardens with beautiful view.
✉ **Llanrwst Road (A470), Llansanffraid Glan Conwy, southeast of Conwy** ☎ **01492 580611** Ⓒ **Closed Christmas and Jan**

Church Bay, Anglesey
Lobster Pot Restaurant (££)
Atmospheric restaurant by a beautiful bay, specialising in fish dishes.
✉ **Church Bay**
☎ **01407 730241**

Criccieth
Moelwyn Restaurant (££)
Award-winning Victorian restaurant with a view of Cardigan Bay and the Cambrian Mountains.
✉ **27–29 Mona Terrace**
☎ **01766 522500**

Deganwy, nr Conwy
Paysanne Restaurant (££)
Provincial French cooking in award-winning and often recommended restaurant.
✉ **Station Road, Deganwy, north of Conwy**
☎ **01492 583848**

Dolgellau
Dylanwad Da (££)
Small, informal restaurant, specialising in Welsh dishes, including lamb.

✉ 2 Ffos-y-Felin
☎ 1341 422870

Harlech
Castle Cottage (££)
Cosy restaurant with authentic cottage look. Traditional Welsh as well as general British dishes, made from fresh, local ingredients.
✉ Pen Lech ☎ 01766 780479
🕐 Closed Feb

Llanberis
Y Bistro (££–£££)
Popular, recommended bistro in Llanberis. Extensive menu, which is changed often.
✉ 43–45 Stryd Fawr
☎ 01286 871278
🕐 No Sunday lunches

Llandudno
Martin's Restaurant (££–£££)
Gourmet establishment in central location near theatre and boulevard.
✉ 11 Mostyn Avenue
☎ 01492 870070

Richard's Bistro Restaurant (££)
Well-known restaurant with guaranteed quality. Everything home-cooked with local ingredients.
✉ 7 Church Walks
☎ 01492 877924

Llandudno Junction
Queen's Head (££)
Busy, comfortable country pub, with traditional Welsh dishes (lamb, fish, game and soup) on the menu.
✉ Glanwydden, Llandudno Junction (B5115)
☎ 01492 546570

Maentwrog
The Grapes (£–££)
Atmospheric, traditional village inn, beautifully situated with walled garden and views from the terrace.
✉ On the A496

Portmeirion
Portmeirion Hotel (£££)
Superb restaurant in luxury hotel, which is part of the fantasy village built in Italianate style. British and Welsh cuisine.
✉ Near Minffordd, via the A487 ☎ 01766 770228

Pwllheli, Lleyn Peninsula
Plas Bodegroes (£££)
Stylish modern British cuisine in elegant ambience. The fish dishes are worth trying.
✉ On the A497 in the direction of Nefyn ☎ 01758 612363
🕐 Closed Nov–Mar

Talyllyn
Tynycornel Hotel (££–£££)
Hotel and restaurant with fine location on the Talyllyn lake, serving high-quality meals.
✉ On the A487 Dolgellau–Tywyn ☎ 01654 782282

Trefriw, Vale of Conwy
Chandler's (££)
Friendly place offering simple meals.
✉ On the B5106
☎ 01492 640991
🕐 Fri dinner and lunch, Wed, Thu and Sat lunch

Tyn-y-Groes
Groes Inn (££)
This traditional, atmospheric inn is a perfect place for eating or drinking (lunch, tea, dinner).
✉ On the B5106, in the Vale of Conwy

Pub Opening Times
Pubs in Wales are open from Monday to Saturday 11AM–11PM. There are, however, still some establishments that close in the afternoon, especially in the countryside (typically 2:30–6:30PM). Sunday opening times are 12AM–10:30PM. There are plans to extend pub opening hours.

Central Wales

**Bara Brith
(speckled bread)**
This traditional Welsh fruit loaf is made as follows: soak 450 grams of dried fruit (or raisins) in 300 millilitres of tea. The following day, add two tablespoons of marmalade, one beaten egg, six tablespoons of brown sugar, one teaspoon of mixed spice, and 450 grams of self-raising flour. Mix. Grease a bread tin and bake for 1¾ hours at 170°C. Leave to cool for at least five minutes, then glaze with honey.

Aberaeron
Hive on the Quay (££)
Friendly restaurant, excellent for lunch or tea; also for dinner in the summer.
✉ **Cadwgan Place** ☎ **01545 570445** ⊘ **Closed end Sep–May**

Aberystwyth
Halfway Inn (£–££)
Vale of Rheidol pub with old-fashioned character. Beautiful views. Special events in summer, such as sheep shearing and live music.
✉ **On the A4120, Pisgah**
☎ **01970 880631**

Brechfa
Ty Mawr Restaurant & Country Hotel (££–£££)
Frequent award-winner and often-recommended eating establishment. Rustic setting.
✉ **Northeast of Carmarthen, near Brechfa Forest**
☎ **01267 202332**

Crickhowell
Nantyffin Cider Mill Inn (£–££)
A 16th-century stone cider mill in a beautiful location beside the Usk. Excellent reputation for tasty and imaginative dishes, including pies, game and fish.
✉ **2.5km (1.5 miles) northwest of Crickhowell, near the junction of the A40 and A479**
☎ **01873 810775**
⊘ **Closed Mon in low season and some weeks in Jan**

Devil's Bridge
Hafod Arms Hotel (££)
Charming country hotel with a view across the Mynach Falls and a wooded ravine. Traditional Welsh cuisine. Also suitable for afternoon tea.
✉ **Near the famous triple bridge** ☎ **01970 890232**

Llwyndafydd
Crown Inn (£–££)
Attractive inn of 18th-century origin near the hidden Cwm valley. Popular with families. Beautiful garden. Play area.
✉ **Near New Quay, via the A486** ☎ **01545 560396**

Llandeilo
Ty Pelan Restaurant (££)
Excellent food in an informal atmosphere. Wide choice of home-made specialities.
✉ **The Old School**
☎ **015558 822644**

Llandrindod Wells
Llanerch Inn
A 16th-century inn in a central location, serving tasty dishes.
✉ **Llanerch Lane**
☎ **01597 822086**

Llangrannog
Ship Inn (£)
Characterful pub with extensive bar-food menu.
✉ **Near the beach**
☎ **01239 654423**

Llanwrtyd Wells
Drovers Restaurant & Tearooms (££)
Attractive, historic restaurant for lunch or dinner in a popular spa town.
✉ **The Square**
☎ **01591 610264**

Rhosmaen, nr Llandeilo
Plough Inn (££)
Known locally for its good cuisine, this inn has Italian owners. Mainly Welsh cuisine and a choice of game dishes.
✉ **On the A40**
☎ **01558 823431**

Southwest Wales

Cynwyl Elfed
The Old Cornmill Restaurant (££)
Cosy restaurant in Welsh cottage style. Beautifully situated on the river.
✉ **In the village of Cynwyl Elfed, north of Carmarthen (A484)**
☎ **01267 281610**

Lamphey
The Dial Inn (£–££)
Close to Pembroke, Carew and the Pembrokeshire Coast Path. Bar meals and a restaurant; the former offers Welsh cawl (lamb broth).
✉ **Ridgeway Road**
☎ **01646 672426**

Laugharne
The Cors Restaurant (££)
Small, elegant restaurant with a private landscaped garden.
✉ **Newbridge Road**
☎ **01994 427219**

Llanddarog
Butcher's Arms (£)
Small country pub with an extensive and varied menu. Favourably located for the National Botanic Garden of Wales.
✉ **Llanddarog is on the B4310, south of the A48**
☎ **01267 275330**

Mabws Fawr, Mathry
The Farmhouse Kitchen (££)
Well-known and often-recommended restaurant with classic cuisine. Extensive wine list.
✉ **Near Mathry, via the A487**
☎ **01348 831347**

Nantgaredig
Four Seasons Restaurant (££)
Restaurant of the Cwmtwrch Farm Hotel. Informal atmosphere. Owners also have a wine shop.
✉ **East of Carmarthen on the A40 to Llandeilo**
☎ **01267 290238**

Nevern
Trewern Arms (£–££)
Characterful 16th-century inn, situated by the Afon Nyfer in one of Pembrokeshire's prettiest villages. Uncomplicated but tasty food.
✉ **On the B4582**
☎ **01239 820395**

Newport (Dyfed)
Cnapen Restaurant (££)
One of the most recommended restaurants in the southwest. Good place for lunch, tea and dinner. Also vegetarian dishes.
✉ **East Street, Newport**
☎ **01239 820575**

Porthgain
Harbour Lights (££)
Small restaurant in cottage style near the sea and St David's. Welsh cuisine.
✉ **In the hamlet of Porthgain**
☎ **01348 831549**

St David's
Morgan's Brasserie (£££)
Fresh fish is an important part of the menu. Also Welsh dishes with beef, lamb and game as their main ingredients.
✉ **20 Nun Street**
☎ **01437 720508**

Pembroke Ferry
Ferry Inn (£–££)
Inn by the Daugleddau. Known for its fish dishes.
✉ **Near Pembroke Dock**
☎ **01646 682947**

Welsh Rarebit
This is probably the best-known dish from Wales. It is very simple to prepare: mix 100 grams of grated mature cheese, 25 grams of butter, three tablespoons of milk (or beer), salt, pepper and a teaspoon of mustard in a saucepan, and heat gently, stirring all the time. Pour the hot mixture over four buttered slices of toast, and pop them under the grill to brown.

South Wales

Cockles

The coast of south Wales is known for its cockles. These small shellfish used to be gathered on the shore by housewives, then washed in seawater and taken home in baskets. These days you can buy cockles in their shells from a fishmonger. Cockles are often preserved in brine, so they need to be rinsed well before cooking. The city of Swansea, in particular, is well known for its cockles. They can be bought in the covered daily market. The cockle festival is one of the highlights of the year.

Cardiff

Blas ar Cymru (££)
Traditional dishes from all parts of Wales in a pleasant setting.
🖂 **48 Crwys Road, Cathays district** ☎ **029 20382132**

La Brasserie, Champers, Le Monde (££)
A combination of atmospheric, lively restaurants with a choice of excellent fish and meat dishes. La Brasserie and Le Monde are French orientated and Champers offers Spanish food.
🖂 **60 St Mary's Street**
☎ **La Brasserie: 029 20372164; Champers: 029 20373363; Le Monde: 029 20387376**

Celtic Cauldron (£)
A friendly daytime café opposite the main entrance of the castle. The menu has a great variety of simple Welsh dishes. Also suitable for vegetarians.
🖂 **Castle Arcade**
☎ **029 20387185**

Cowbridge

Off the Beaten Track (£–££)
Recommended atmospheric stopping place for lunch, tea or dinner in small town between Bridgend and Cardiff.
🖂 **1 Town Hall Square**
☎ **01446 773599**

Dinas Powys, nr Cardiff

The Huntsman (£–££)
A friendly, authentically furnished country inn not far from Cardiff. Welsh and British cuisine.
🖂 **Station Road, Dinas Powys, between Penarth and Barry**
☎ **029 20514900**

Merthyr Tydfil

Nant Ddu Lodge Hotel (££)
Guests have a choice of bar or bistro. Ever-changing menu, specialising in regional dishes made with fresh ingredients.
🖂 **10km (6 miles) north of Merthyr on the A470**
☎ **01685 379111**

Reynoldston, Gower

Fairyhill (£££)
This frequently recommended country house hotel is an oasis of peace in the heart of the Gower peninsula. The imaginatively prepared food is not cheap, but is certainly value for money.
🖂 **Northwest of Reynoldston, 20 minutes from junction 47 of the M4, via the B4295**
☎ **01792 390139**

St George's, nr Cardiff

The Greendown Inn (£–££)
Cosy, 15th-century inn in rural surroundings, not far from the capital. Traditional British cuisine.
🖂 **Drope Road, St George's, accessible from junction 33 of the M4**
☎ **01446 760310**

Swansea

Number One Wind Street (£££)
Contemporary restaurant with both French and Welsh dishes on the menu.
🖂 **1 Wind Street**
☎ **01792 456996**

Creigiau

Ceasar's Arms (££)
Country pub with excellent food. Also for fish lovers.
🖂 **13km (8 miles) northwest of Cardiff city centre**
☎ **01222 890486**

The Borderlands

Berriew
Lion Hotel (££)
Traditional village hotel of 17th-century origin with black-and-white timber framing. There is a choice of eating in the bar or restaurant.
✉ In the village centre near the church
☎ 01686 640452

Clytha,
nr Abergavenny
Clytha Arms (££)
Characterful village inn with informal atmosphere. Regional dishes, including fish. Eat in the bar or the restaurant.
✉ In the village
☎ 01873 840206

Hay-on-Wye
Old Black Lion (£–££)
A 17th-century inn with good cuisine. Wide-ranging choice, both in the bar and restaurant.
✉ 26 Lion Street
☎ 01497 820841

Howey,
nr Llandrindod Wells
Drovers Arms (£)
Rustic inn in a pretty village. Local dishes made with fresh ingredients are served in the bar or à la carte in the restaurant.
✉ In the village, accessible via the A483
☎ 01597 822508

Llanfyllin
Seeds Restaurant (££)
Small, intimate restaurant with Welsh cuisine. Menu varies according to season. Suitable for lunch, tea and dinner.
✉ 5 Penbryn Cottages, High Street
☎ 01691 648604

Llanfihangel-Nant-Melan,
nr New Radnor
Red Lion Inn (£–££)
Both traditional Welsh and modern dishes are on the menu at this friendly, historic cattle-drivers' inn.
✉ On the A44
☎ 01544 350220

Llangollen
Gales (£)
Bistro-style establishment with church pews. Delicious home-made dishes for relatively little money. Excellent wine cellar.
✉ 18 Bridge Street
☎ 01978 860089

Newtown
Yesterday's Restaurant (£)
Restaurant in the centre with a wide choice, including lamb and vegetarian dishes.
✉ Severn Square
☎ 01686 622644

Trelleck,
nr Monmouth
Village Green (££)
Unusual pub and restaurant, housed in a 16th-century building that once belonged to a monastery. Traditional bar food in the pub and more internationally orientated à-la-carte dishes in the restaurant.
✉ On the B4293 south of Monmouth ☎ 01600 860119

Whitebrook,
Wye Valley
The Crown at Whitebrook (££–£££)
Renowned restaurant in a small valley, 2km (1 mile) from the Wye. Provincial French cuisine.
✉ Between Monmouth and Tintern ☎ 01600 860254

Laver Bread
Laver is a fine, soft kind of seaweed, which is found on the south coast and is very edible. Sold in local shops and supermarkets, it needs to be rinsed extremely well before preparation, and then cooked for five to six hours. After drying, it is mixed with oatmeal, making a thick paste.
The laver bread can be eaten in many different ways: hot with melted butter, salt, pepper and lemon juice on toast; baked with bacon on toast; cold with vinegar, or mixed with orange juice as an accompaniment to lamb.

North Wales

Hotel Prices

A double bedroom with breakfast costs approximately:

£   = less than £50
££   = £50–£75
£££   = £75–£100
££££ = more than £100

Staying at The Lighthouse

A Victorian lighthouse (1862), which was used until 1985, is a rare address at which to stay. The location, high on the rocks of Great Ormes Head near Llandudno, is second to none. There are three rooms available – reserve well in advance (££–£££).

✉ The Lighthouse, Marina Drive
☎ 01492 876819, fax 01492 876668,
e-mail enquiries@lighthouse-llandudno.co.uk,
www.lighthouse-llandudno.co.uk

Aberdyfi
Penhelig Arms (£££)

White 18th-century inn with view across the Dyfi and the sea. Excellent cuisine.

✉ Near the railway station
☎ 01654 767215, fax 01654 767690, e-mail
penheligarms@saqnet.co.uk

Abersoch, Lleyn Peninsula
Porth Tocyn Country House Hotel (£££)

Cosy hotel in quiet environs with views across Cardigan Bay. Also suitable for guests with children. Good restaurant. Swimming pool.

✉ 1km (½ mile) south of Abersoch, via Sarn Bach and Bwlchtocyn
☎ 01758 713303, fax 01758 713538
🅾 Easter–Oct

Beddgelert
Sygun Fawr Country House Hotel (££)

Characterful 17th-century manor house situated within the mountain heart of Snowdonia. Suitable starting point for walks and climbs.

✉ Just outside Beddgelert, on the A498 to Capel Curig
☎ 01766 890258 (phone/fax)

Buduan, Lleyn Peninsula
The Old Rectory (££)

Small, tastefully furnished guest house in an old rectory. Informal atmosphere. View of the garden and village church. Central location for exploring the Lleyn peninsula.

✉ Between Pwllheli and Morfa Nefyn
☎ 01758 721519

Capel Garmon, nr Betws-y-coed
White Horse Inn (££)

Friendly, unassuming village inn, originally 16th century. Within walking distance of the tourist resort of Beddgelert.

✉ In the hamlet of Capel Garmon
☎ 01690 710271 (phone/fax)

Cenmaes, nr Machynlleth
Penrhos Arms Hotel (££)

Picturesque inn in a small, rural village. Excellent quality, both in terms of rooms and service.

✉ In Cenmaes on the A470
☎ 01650 511243

Llandudno
Belle Vue Hotel (££)

Unpretentious but good family hotel. Comfortable rooms and hospitable reception. Central location on the seafront.

✉ 26 North Parade
☎ 01492 879547, fax 01492 870001

St Tudno Hotel (££££)

Fairly small, stylish seaside hotel, housed in a Victorian building on the sea front. Luxurious interior and excellent restaurant.

✉ 16 North Parade, near pier and beach
☎ 01492 874411, fax 01492 860407, e-mail
sttudnohotel@btinternet.com

Meantwrog, nr Blaenau Ffestiniog
Grapes Hotel (££)

Old mail-coach stopping place in a central location. Hospitable and atmospheric, with good food.

✉ In the hamlet of Meantwrog, via the A496
☎ 01766 590365, fax 590654

Menai Bridge, Anglesey
Wern Farm (£–££)

Very comfortable

accommodation in a farm dating from 1600. Surrounded by fields (cows and sheep). Limited number of rooms.

⊠ Pentreath Road, Menai Bridge ☎ 01248 712421 (phone/fax), e-mail brayshaw_ wernfarm@compuserve.com

Pass of Llanberis, nr Nantgwynant
Pen-y-Gwryd (£)
Simple, straightforward inn set in a solitary location in the heart of Snowdonia. Popular with walkers and climbers.

⊠ At the junction of the A498 and A4086 ☎ 01286 870211

Portmeirion
Gwesty Portmeirion Hotel (££££)
Luxurious hotel, beautifully situated by the Treath Bach estuary, in the village built in Italian style by Clough Williams-Ellis.

⊠ In Portmeirion, southeast of Porthmadog ☎ 01766 770000, fax 01766 771331, e-mail hotel@portmeirion-wales.com

Red Wharf Bay, Anglesey
Bryn Tirion Hotel (££–£££)
Located on a spacious bay, this family hotel has a beautiful view and private garden.

⊠ On Red Wharf Bay ☎ 01248 852366, fax 01248 852013

Rhostryfan, nr Caernarfon
Hafoty (£–££)
Excellent farmhouse accommodation. Good views of Caernarfon, the Menai Strait and Anglesey.

⊠ 7km (4½ miles) south of Caernarfon via the A487

☎ 01286 830144, fax 01286 830441

Seion, Llanddeiniolen
Ty'n Rhos (££–£££)
Converted farm in a rural location. Excellent rooms and good cuisine.

⊠ Between Bangor and Caernarfon ☎ 01248 670489, fax 01248 670079, e-mail enquiries@tynrhos.co.uk

Talsarnau, nr Harlech
Gwrach Ynys Country Guest House (£)
Spacious and comfortably furnished guest house in a rural location. Limited number of rooms.

⊠ North of Harlech via the A496 ☎ 01766 780742, fax 01766 781199

Tal-y-llyn
Minffordd Hotel (££–£££)
Fairly simple, but atmospheric, hospitable hotel. Beautifully location in the foothills of Cader Idris.

⊠ Near the Tal-y-llyn lake, close to the junction of the A487 and B4405 ☎ 01654 761665, fax 01654 761517, e-mail info@minffordd.com ◉ Closed Jan to mid-Mar

Trefriw, Vale of Conwy
Hafod Country Hotel (££)
17th-century farm converted to a hotel. Small, but comfortably furnished establishment with an old-fashioned atmosphere.

⊠ In the hamlet of Trefriw on the B5106, on the west side of the Vale of Conwy ☎ 01492 640029, fax 01492 641351

Visitors with Disabilities
Hotels, guest houses and B&Bs can be inspected for their suitability for wheelchair users. One of the three following symbols can be assigned: a wheelchair on its own (establishment suitable for wheelchair users travelling alone); a wheelchair with assistant; and the symbol of a standing man with stick (only suitable for wheelchair users who can take a few steps and can walk up three steps). Information:
Holiday Care Service Imperial Buildings, Victoria Road, Horley RH6 7PZ, UK ☎ 01293 774535.

Central Wales

Bed and Breakfast (B&B)

One form of accommodation that is popular in Wales is a stay in a private house. A generous cooked breakfast is included. Although prices have increased in recent years, B&Bs are still considerably cheaper than hotels. The Welsh Tourist Board (WTB) issues the annually updated *Bed and Breakfast Touring Map* with some 160 addresses. The brochure *Wales Farm Holidays* lists farms which offer bed and breakfast.

Aberaeron

Hazeldene (£)

The guest house occupies a spacious, elegant town house built in 1906. Good service from the friendly owners. Limited number of rooms.

✉ **South Road** ☎ **01545 570652, fax 01545 571012, e-mail hazeldeneaberaeron@teco.net**

Aberystwyth

Aberystwyth Park Lodge (£–££)

Modern hotel complex opened summer 2000. Excellent facilities. Close to the town centre and attractions.

✉ **Parc-y-Lleyn** ☎ **01970 625588 (phone/fax)**

Brecon

Castle Hotel of Brecon (££)

This one-time late-18th-century inn is now a fairly large town hotel overlooking the River Usk. It stands on the site of the medieval castle (some ruins).

✉ **The Avenue, near the town centre** ☎ **01874 624611, fax 01874 623737, e-mail hotel@breconcastle.co.uk**

Cardigan

Pentbrontbren (£££)

Attractive accommodation in a renovated farm. Tastefully furnished rooms. Excellent cuisine.

✉ **North of Cardigan, between Tan-y-Groes and Glynarthen** ☎ **01239 810248, fax 01239 811129**

Crickhowell

The Bear Hotel (£££)

Historic coaching inn with a strong reputation for atmosphere, comfort and service. One of the most characteristic inns in Wales.

✉ **In the centre of the town** ☎ **01873 810408, fax 01873 811696**

Cwm Taf, nr Merthyr Tydfill

Nant Ddu Lodge Hotel (££–£££)

Georgian-style hotel in the middle of the Brecon Beacons National Park. Excellent accommodation and service.

✉ **On the A470 Merthyr Tydfil–Brecon** ☎ **01685 379111, fax 01685 377088**

Dardy, nr Crickhowell

Ty Croeso Hotel (££)

Small hotel set on a wooded hill above the Usk Valley. Relaxed atmosphere, justifying its name 'House of Welcome'. Taste-of-Wales cuisine.

✉ **1km (½ mile) west of Crickhowell via the B4568** ☎ **01873 810573 (phone/fax), e-mail tycroeso@tycroeso-hotel.freeserve.co.uk**

Howey, nr Llandrindod Wells

Brynhir Farm (££)

Characteristic 17th-century house, part of a working farm. Very good facilities. This is particularly suitable for walkers and birdwatchers.

✉ **Chapel Road, Howey, 3km (2 miles) south of Llandrindod Wells** ☎ **01597 822425 (phone/fax)**

Lampeter

Dremddu Fawr Farm (£)

An Edwardian farmhouse B&B in a rural location. Home-cooked evening meals by arrangement.

✉ **6.5km (4 miles) north of**

Lampeter off the A482 road to Aberaeron ☎ 01570 470394

Llandrindod Wells
Llanerch Inn (££)
Friendly town inn of 16th-century origin, with good accommodation and cuisine. Also suitable for families.

✉ Llanerch Lane, in the centre of Llandrindod Wells ☎ 01597 822086, fax 01597 824618

Llangorse, nr Brecon
Red Lion Hotel (££)
An 18th-century village inn with good rooms and cuisine. Garden looks out towards Llangorse Lake.

✉ In Llangorse, opposite the church ☎ 01874 658238, fax 01874 658595

Llanwrda, nr Llandeilo
Glanrannell Park Hotel (£££)
Comfortable hotel, set in a rural location in private parkland with a lake, surrounded by hills. Popular area for nature lovers.

✉ In Llanwrda on the A40 between Llandovery and Llandeilo ☎ 01558 685230, fax 01558 685784

Ⓒ Closed winter months

Llyswen
Griffin (££–£££)
An attractive, old-fashioned inn in the Upper Wye Valley. Possibly dating from 1467. Relaxed atmosphere. Good base for an activity holiday (walking, angling, horse riding). Excellent restaurant (fish and game).

✉ In Llyswyn (A470) between Brecon and Builth Wells ☎ 01874 754241, fax 01874 754592

Manordeilo, nr Llandeilo
Brynteilo Guest House (£)
Guest house in a rural location. Modern and unpretentious, with simple furnishings. The hostess is well known as a chef on regional television.

✉ In Manordeilo on the A40 between Llandovery and Llandeilo ☎ 01550 777040, fax 01550 777884

Penybont, nr Llandrindod Wells
Severn Arms Hotel (££)
Former mail-coach stop. Comfortable rooms and very good restaurant.

✉ Near the junction of the A44 and A488 ☎ 01597 851224, fax 01597 851693

Talybont-on-Usk
Usk Inn (££)
Originally a simple village inn, transformed by the present owners into a country hotel with excellent facilities.

✉ In Talybont-on-Usk, south-east of Brecon ☎ 01874 676251, fax 01874 676392, e-mail stay@uskinn.co.uk

Three Cocks, nr Talgarth
Three Cocks Hotel (££)
Characterful historic inn. It has a renowned cuisine with obvious Belgian influences.

✉ On the northern edge of the Black Mountains, northeast of Brecon on the A438 ☎ 01497 847215, fax 01497 847339

Southwest Wales

Youth Hostels
The Youth Hostel Association has some 40, often beautifully situated, houses in Wales, which are open to older as well as young people. They are often convenient stopping places for walking tours along the coast or through the mountains. Information from: Youth Hostel Association Trevelyan House, 8 St Stephen's Hill, St Albans AL1 2DY
☎ 01727 845047, e-mail customerservices @yha.org.uk, www.yha.org.uk

Cosheston, nr Pembroke
Poyerston Farm (£–££)
Charming, Victorian farm with a pretty garden. Good quality accommodation and cuisine.
✉ **Northeast of Pembroke off the A47** ☎ **01646 651347 (phone/fax)**

Gwaun Valley
Tregynon Country Farmhouse Hotel (££–£££)
This solitary 16th-century farm offers visitors plenty of peace and quiet. Good base for walking. Meals prepared with care.
✉ **In the Gwaun Valley, via the B4313** ☎ **01239 820531, fax 01239 820808, e-mail tregynon@online-holidays.net**

Llandeloy, nr Solva
Lochmeyler Farm Guest House (£)
Excellent quality farm accommodation, at a short distance of St David's. Bedrooms in main building and in adjacent cottages.
✉ **Just outside the village of Llandeloy** ☎ **01348 837724, fax 01348 837622**

St David's
St Non's Hotel (££–£££)
Friendly hotel in a central location. It dates back to a 13th-century hostelry for pilgrims. Stylish interior and an excellent restaurant.
✉ **On the southern edge of the city centre** ☎ **01437 720239, fax 01437 721839, e-mail stnons@enterprise.net**
🕘 **Closed Nov–Dec**

Warpool Court Hotel (££££)
Luxurious, spacious and historic hotel in the former Cathedral Choir School. Unique location with beautiful views above St Non's Bay.
✉ **South of St David's**
☎ **01437 720300, fax 01437 720676, e-mail warpool@enterprise.net**
🕘 **Closed Jan**

Spittal
Lower Haytong Farmhouse (£–££)
This characteristic – originally 13th-century – working farm offers comfortably furnished rooms and good food.
✉ **8km (5 miles) north of Haverfordwest** ☎ **01437 731279 (phone/fax)**

Tenby
Broadmead Hotel (£–££)
Comfortable hotel occupying an attractive 18th-century country house. Semi-rural location at walking distance from the town centre. Good facilities and food.
✉ **Heywood Lane** ☎ **01834 842641, fax 01834 845757**

Heywood Lodge Country House Hotel (£££)
Elegant and luxuriously furnished Victorian country house in private parkland. High-quality service and food. Not suitable for children. Limited number of rooms.
✉ **Heywood Lane** ☎ **01834 842684, fax 01834 843976**

Wolfscastle
Wolfscastle Country Hotel (£££)
Attractive country-house style hotel in the heart of Pembrokeshire. Relaxed, hospitable atmosphere. Good cuisine.
✉ **Between Fishguard and Haverfordwest on the A40** ☎ **01437 741225, fax 01437 741383, e-mail andy741225@aol.com**

South Wales

Abercraf
Maes-y-Gwernen Hotel
A friendly, small hotel where guests receive a good, personal service.
✉ **Abercraf, in the Upper Tawe Valley on the southwest edge of the Brecon Beacons National Park** ☎ **01639 730218, fax 01639 730765, e-mail maesyg@globalnet.co.uk**

Cardiff
Cardiff Bay Hotel (££££)
Very luxurious modern hotel on Cardiff Bay. Wide range of facilities. Renowned cuisine.
✉ **Schooner Way, Atlantic Wharf, Cardiff Bay** ☎ **029 20475000**

Greendown Inn (£££)
A 15th-century inn just outside Cardiff, close to the Welsh Folk Museum. Comfortable rooms and good cuisine.
✉ **Drope Road, St George's** ☎ **01446 760310 (phone/fax)**

Lincoln House (££)
An attractive Victorian style hotel in the city centre. Convenient location near the main sights. Reasonably priced.
✉ **118 Cathedral Road** ☎ **029 20395558, fax 029 20230537**

The Town House (££)
One of the best bed-and-breakfast establishments in Cardiff. The Town House occupies a favourable location just a ten-minute walk from the city centre.
✉ **70 Cathedral Road** ☎ **029 20239399, fax 20223214, e-mail thetownhouse@msn.com**

Langland, Gower
Langland Court (££££)
Elegant late Victorian hotel with a splendid garden. Great care is taken over the food.
✉ **Langland Court Road** ☎ **01792 361545, fax 01792 362302, e-mail info@langlandcourthotel.co.uk**

Parkmill, Gower
Parc Le Breos House (£)
Spacious 18th-century farm in the heart of the beautiful landscape of the Gower peninsula. Fairly simple, but hospitable establishment.
✉ **Parkmill** ☎ **01792 371636, fax 01792 371287**

Reynoldston, Gower
King Arthur Hotel (££)
Picturesque, rural inn on Reynoldston Common. Traditional village pub atmosphere. Friendly reception. Popular restaurant.
✉ **Higher Green** ☎ **01792 391099**

St Fagans
Scotts of St Fagans (££–£££)
The former village post office of this attractive commuter town has been transformed into a tasteful hotel with modern furnishings. The interior looks more Scandinavian than Welsh. Very good restaurant.
✉ **Centre of St Fagans** ☎ **029 20565400, fax 029 20563400**

Swansea
Windsor Lodge Hotel (£££)
Characterful, originally 18th-century hotel in the city centre. Good facilities.
✉ **Mount Pleasant** ☎ **01792 642158, fax 01792 648996**

Rating System
Inspected accommodation in Wales is rated from one to five stars. These refer to location, amenities, interior, service and atmosphere. The stars are further refined in the categories hotel, inn, farm, guest house and B&B. A distinction is made between holiday parks (with site caravans), touring parks (mobile caravans and tents), and camping parks (tents). Cottages and other holiday homes are rated from one to five ticks.

The Borderlands

Staying in a Former Priory

The Abbey Hotel (££) in the unsurpassed Vale of Ewyas forms part of the substantial and evocative ruins of Llanthony Priory, one of the most inspiring locations in Britain. The inn occupies the former prior's dwelling.

Hotel Prices

Hotels in Britain can be expensive. You may be able to take advantage of reduced prices through tour operators or special seasonal offers. Ask your travel agent for details.

Berriew, nr Welshpool
Lion Hotel (£££)

Characterful, 17th-century timber-framed inn in a pretty village. Small, but comfortably furnished rooms. Good food.

⊠ In the village centre, next to the church ☎ 01686 640452, fax 01686 640604

Chepstow
Castle View (££–£££)

An 18th-century inn, opposite one of Wales's best-known castles.

⊠ 16 Bridge Street ☎ 01291 620349, fax 01291 627397, e-mail mart@castview.demon.co.uk

Crossgates, nr Llandrindod Wells
Guidfa House (££)

Friendly and comfortable Georgian-style guest house.

⊠ Near the junction of the A44 and A483 ☎ 01597 851241, fax 01597 851875, e-mail guidfa@globalnet.co.uk

Knighton
Milebrook House Hotel (£££)

Fine 18th-century country-house hotel, situated on the English border and Offa's Dyke Path. Emphasis on comfort, good food and an informal atmosphere.

⊠ In Milebrook, just outside Knighton on the A4113 road to Ludlow ☎ 01547 582632, fax 01547 520509, e-mail hotel@milebrook.kc3ltd.co.uk

Llanarmon Dyffryn Ceiriog
West Arms Hotel (£££)

A charming 17th-century inn in a remote village on the eastern side of the Berwyn mountain range. Friendly establishment.

⊠ Southwest of Chirk, at the end of the B4500 ☎ 01691 600665, fax 01691 600622

Llangollen
Fron Deg (£–££)

Excellent B&B address in this pleasant festival town. Carefully chosen interior.

⊠ Abbey Road ☎ 01978 860126, fax 01978 860456, e-mail frondeg @llanpaget.freeserve.co.uk

Montgomery
Dragon Hotel (££–£££)

Hotel built in timber-framed style typical of the region. Located in a historic town. Excellent restaurant.

⊠ Montgomery town centre ☎ 01686 668359, fax 01686 668287, e-mail Dragon_Michaels @compuserve.com

Presteigne
Radnorshire Arms (£££)

One of the most renowned inns in the border area. Eminent example of black-and-white timber-framing from 1616. the authentic interior provides a cosy atmosphere.

⊠ Between Knighton and Kington on the B4355 ☎ 01544 267406, fax 01544 260418

Tintern
Parva Farmhouse Hotel (££–£££)

The guest house, converted from 17th-century farm, is one of the best in the region. Careful attention to comfort, service and atmosphere. Award-winning restaurant.

⊠ In the Wye Valley, a short distance from Tintern Abbey ☎ 01291 689411/689511, fax 01291 689557

Craft Shops and Woollen Mills

North Wales

Afonwen Craft and Antique Centre
Large craft centre on the north side of the Clwydian Range. Also antiques.
- ✉ B5122
- ☎ 01352 720965

Beddgelert Woodcraft Gallery
Clocks, barometers, paintings and other exhibits.
- ✉ Minafon, Beddgelert
- ☎ 01766 890586

Brynkir Woollen Mill
Visitors can follow the entire production process. There is also a shop on the site.
- ✉ Golan, nr Tremadog
- ☎ 01766 530236

Canolfan y Celfyddydau
Part of the Aberystwyth Arts Centre. Workshop, exhibition and shop.
- ✉ University campus (via A487), 1.5km (1 mile) outside Aberystwyth centre
- ☎ 01970 622895

Glyn Llifon
Workshops in the rustic surroundings of a country park.
- ✉ Southwest of Caernarfon, in the direction of Dinas Dinlle, via the A487 and A499
- ☎ 01286 830232

Inigo Jones Slate Works
A quarry since 1861. Visitors can see how all kinds of slate items are made.
- ✉ In Groeslon, near Nantlle
- ☎ 01286 830242

James Pringle Weavers
Popular outlet for all kinds of woollen items and crafts. Very big and busy.
- ✉ In the centre of Llanfair PG, Anglesey
- ☎ 01248 717171

Mirage Glass
Glass objects and stained glass
- ✉ Llangedwyn Mill, Llangedwyn, nr Oswestry
- ☎ 01691 780618

Oriel Mostyn Art Gallery
International contemporary arts and crafts. The museum also has a Wales Crafts Council shop.
- ✉ 12 Vaughan Street, Llandudno ☎ 1492 879201

Oriel Ynys Mon
The most important craft gallery in Anglesey.
- ✉ Llangefni, Anglesey
- ☎ 01248 724444

Padarn Country Park Craft Shops
A number of craft workshops, where artists demonstrate their skills to the public, are part of the park.
- ✉ Padarn Country Park, Llanberis
- ☎ 01286 870892

Penmachno Woollen Mill
One of the best-known woollen mills in Wales. You can see the weavers at work.
- ✉ Just north of the village on the B4406

Ruthin Craft Centre
Several different, independent workshops are brought together under one roof.
- ✉ In Ruthin, on the western edge of the Clwydian Range
- ☎ 01824 703992/1704774

Woollen Mills
There are many woollen mills across Wales. In some cases, such as Pringle in Llanfair PG, and Meirion in Dinas Mawddwy, these are actually stores specialising in woollen items. Visitors who also wish to see the production process can choose from Brynkir, Penmachno, Trefriw and Tregwynt.

Wales Craft Council

An umbrella organisation with many craftspeople as members. They are allowed to use the yellow daffodil emblem and label, which guarantees that the article is made in Wales. The WCC organises a number of large craft markets every year and provides information on where to buy certain items.
☎ 01938 555313,
fax 01938 556237.

Snowdon Mill

A range of crafts under one roof.
✉ Porthmadog

The Chapel Art

Exhibition of high-quality crafts, made by local, regional, national and international artists.
✉ 8 Marine Crescent, near the castle, Criccieth
☎ 01766 523570

The White Room Gallery

Ceramics and other craft products in an attractive setting.
✉ Harlech Pottery, Pentre Efail, Harlech
☎ 01766 780501

Trefriw Woollen Mill

All parts of the production process are shown during a tour (without guide) of this factory, which is more than 150 years old. There is also a shop with a wide range of goods.
✉ On the main road in the village
☎ 01492 640462

Central Wales

Canolfan Crafft Cymru

Craft shop, also selling jewellery (Celtic design)
✉ On the central square of Tregaron

Clos Pengarreg Courtyard

Different workshops in an old farm complex
✉ Within walking distance of Aberaeron harbour
☎ 01545 570460/571795

Corris Craft Centre

Modern craft centre, consisting of different workshops.
✉ North of Machynlleth on the A487 ☎ 01654 761584

Hay-on-Wye Craft Centre

A number of craft workshops, brought together in one centre.
✉ By the central car park in Hay-on-Wye

Museum of the Welsh Woollen Industry

The production process of the woollen trade is demonstrated and shown in pictures.
✉ Dre-fach Felindre, nr Llandysul ☎ 01559 370929

Old Station

Former railway station, converted into a shopping centre with clothes and craft shops.
✉ In the centre of Welshpool
☎ 01938 556622

Welsh Gold Shop

Shop with home-produced gold jewellery. The guided tour round the Gwynfynydd Gold Mine, in the Coed-y-Brenin woods north of Dolgellau, departs from here.
✉ In the centre of Dolgellau
☎ 01341 423332

Welsh Royal Crystal

Visitors can see how hand-made crystal is produced. There is also a shop
✉ In Rhayader
☎ 01597 811005

South Wales

Craft in the Bay

A wide selection of crafts, made by members of a craft guild.
✉ 57 Bute Street, Cardiff Bay
☎ 029 20484611

Castle Quarter
Opposite Cardiff Castle entrance are various craft shops, including the Castle Welsh Crafts in Castle Street, and the Welsh Lovespoon Gallery in Castle Arcade.
☎ **Castle Welsh Crafts: 029 20343038;**
Welsh Lovespoon Gallery: 029 20231500

Dinefwr Craft Centre
Various craft shops under one roof in pleasant country town.
✉ **In Llandovery**
☎ **01550 721452**

Ffwrrwm Art and Craft Centre
Arts, crafts and sculpture in a historic town. Shops and café.
✉ **Off High Street, Caerleon**
☎ **01633 430777**

Model House Craft and Design Centre
Artisans show their crafts in this attractive centre. There are also coins on display – Llantrisant is home to the Royal Mint.
✉ **Bull Ring, Llantrisant, northwest of Cardiff via the A4119**
☎ **01443 237758**

Rock Mills (Y Felin Wlan)
The family business has been going for a hundred years. The products are for sale.
✉ **Capel Dewi near Llandysul, via the B4459**

Stuart Crystal
Both the blowing and decorating of crystal can be seen in this factory. There is also a shop.
✉ **Aberbargoed, nr**

Blackwood (Rhymney Valley, A4049)
☎ **01443 820044**

Stuart Crystal
The exhibition highlights modern and older products made by this company. The crystal is for sale.
✉ **Bridge Street, Chepstow**
☎ **01291 620135**

Trapp Art and Crafts Centre
Well-known outlet for arts and crafts.
✉ **In Trapp village, close to Carreg Cennen Castle**
☎ **01269 850362**

Tregwynt Woollen Mill
Welsh woollens are produced and sold in this 18th-century factory.
✉ **Near St Nicolas, west of Fishguard**
☎ **01348 891225**

Wallis Woollen Mill
A 19th-century woollen mill in the vicinity of the attractive Llysyfran Country Park.
✉ **Ambleston, northeast of Haverfordwest** ☎ **01437 731297**

Welsh Crafts
Typical Welsh crafts include: finely carved wooden love spoons, woven fabrics, gold and silver jewellery with Celtic designs, ceramics and porcelain, crystal ware and utensils made from slate.

Good Shopping Cities

Cardiff Shopping Hours
Shops in the centre of the capital are normally open Monday to Saturday 9:30–5:30. Many shops are also open on Sunday 11–5. Thursday is late night shopping, when stores close at 8PM.

North Wales

Llandudno is the most important centre for shopping in north Wales. The main shops are in and around Mostyn Street, Lloyd Street and Gloddaeth Street. There are also stores belonging to the various high street chains.

Bangor, too, has good shopping facilities, particularly in the long High Street, while Colwyn Bay offers a pleasant alternative to those who prefer smaller shops.

Central Wales

Aberystwyth has a good shopping centre in the streets behind the seafront promenade. The high streets of Welshpool, Newtown and Llandrindod Wells are also good for shopping.

South Wales

Carmarthen, Haverfordwest and Tenby are regional centres. If you are not looking for anything exotic, you will find everything here. The big towns in the densely populated Valleys all have large shopping centres, though they lack a certain atmosphere. Cwmbran, Wales's only new town, has an excellent contemporary shopping centre. Near Bridgend, at a short distance from junction 36 of the M4, is the immense McArthurGlen Designer Outlet Centre, with more than 60 shops selling designer clothing at vastly reduced prices. A cinema, playground and restaurants complete the complex.

Swansea

Wales's second city has a large modern shopping area with a wide range of goods. The Quadrant Shopping Centre, the St David's Shopping Centre and Oxford Street are some of the most important parts. They look fairly sterile, however, and lack atmosphere and intimacy. The historic market hall is an exception to this rule.

Cardiff

The capital is not only the best shopping city in the principality but one of the best in Britain. There are large covered shopping centres: St David's Centre, Queens Arcade and the Capitol Centre. In terms of construction and appearance these shopping areas or malls are not much different from similar ones in other British cities.

Cardiff owes its charm as a shopping city mainly to the small Victorian and Edwardian galleries that connect the main thoroughfares. The oldest is the Royal Arcade from 1856; the most beautiful is the Castle Arcade.

The more than 50 stalls of the Central Market are housed in a Victorian hall. David Morgan is the largest department store in Wales and was founded in 1879. Howells is part of House of Fraser. Antiques can be found especially in the Royal Arcade, Jacob's Market and The Pumping Station.

Children's Attractions

North Wales

Alice in Wonderland Centre
Tableaux vivants bring Lewis Carroll's classic story about a little girl's adventures to life.
✉ **3–4 Trinity Square, Llandudno**
☎ **01492 860082**

Anglesey Sea Zoo
A zoo specialising in underwater world.
✉ **Brynsiencyn**
☎ **01248 430411**

Dinosaur World
A collection of some 30 life-size dinosaurs in a reconstructed prehistoric environment.
✉ **Eirias Park, Colwyn Bay**
☎ **01492 518111**

Harlequin Puppet Theatre
Puppet theatre with performances in the afternoon and evening in July, August and other holiday periods.
✉ **Rhos-on-Sea**
☎ **01492 548166**

King Arthur's Labyrinth
An underground boat trip that travels through caves, showing the life of King Arthur.
✉ **Corris Craft Centre near Machynlleth**
☎ **01654 761584**

Llechwedd Slate Caverns
Slate quarry with the underground Deep Mine Tour, where you travel in the carriages once used to transport slate – especially fascinating for children. Old-fashioned school slates and other items for sale.
✉ **Blaenau Ffestiniog**
☎ **01766 830306**

Marquis of Anglesey's Column
A 27m column, which can be climbed for a wide panorama.
✉ **In Llanfair PG**
☎ **01248 714393**

Museum of Childhood
Childhood toys, games, dolls and utensils dating back to the 18th century.
✉ **1 Castle Street, Beaumaris**
☎ **01248 712498**

Ocean Beach Amusement Park
This permanent beach fun fair is an inevitable attraction in this classic seaside resort.
✉ **West Parade, Rhyl**
☎ **01745 343246**

Starcoast
Average theme park and attractive, well-organised subtropical swimming pool.
✉ **East of Pwllheli on the A497** ☎ **01758 701441**

Sun Centre
Family fun in this wonderful swimming paradise – especially when the weather is bad.
✉ **East Parade, Rhyl**
☎ **01745 344433**

Sygun Copper Mine
An underground tour through tunnels and caves is always interesting for children.
✉ **2km (1¼ miles) north of Beddgelert**
☎ **01766 510100**

Welsh Mountain Zoo
A good zoo of reasonable size.
✉ **Colwyn Bay**
☎ **01492 532938**

Castles and Trains
Castles and narrow-gauge railways, with or without steam trains, are among the attractions that always fascinate children. They are not mentioned separately on these pages, as they are listed in detail elsewhere in this guide.

109

Smaller Attractions

Not all attractions are mentioned in these pages. The local tourist offices have information on other sights that are interesting for children. These include parks specialising in particular types of animals (butterflies, farm animals, birds, fish), swimming pools, theme parks, piers, mines, car museums and boat trips.

Central Wales

Dolaucothi Gold Mines

Gold mines founded by the Romans. A guided tour explores the underground tunnels.

✉ **Pumpsaint near Llanwrda**
☎ **01558 650359**

South Wales

Aquadome at the Afon Lido

A swimming paradise with many attractions, including sound effects.

✉ **Aberavon Promenade**
☎ **01639 871444**

Big Pit Mining Museum

A cage lift takes visitors to the shaft network at a depth of 90m, where former miners conduct a guided tour. Some of the tour involves crawling through very low shafts – exciting for the children but not for adults who suffer from back problems.

✉ **Blaenavon, southwest of Abergavenny**
☎ **01495 790311**

Dan-yr-Ogof Showcaves

The largest cave network in western Europe open to visitors. Stalagmites and stalactites are supplemented by other attractions, such as a dinosaur park, cart-horse centre, Iron Age farm, and a museum.

✉ **On the A4067 in the Brecon Beacons National Park**
☎ **01639 730284**

Folly Farm

Large children's farm with many other attractions for younger children.

✉ **On the A478 Tenby–Narberth road**
☎ **01834 812731**

Manor House Wildlife and Leisure Park

A large, attractive zoo, with several theme-park type attractions.

✉ **St Florence, near Tenby**
☎ **01646 651201**

Oakwood Park

The largest theme park in Wales. A single ticket allows access to all the attractions.

✉ **Canaston Bridge, near Narberth**
☎ **01834 891376/891373**

Oceanarium

Good sea aquarium

✉ **St David's**
☎ **01437 720453**

Rhondda Heritage Park

Go with an ex-miner down in the cage lift and experience what it was like to work in the heat and darkness underground.

✉ **Trahefod, near Pontypridd**
☎ **01443 682036**

Swansea Leisure Centre

This complex has a great subtropical swimming pool with slides and a wave pool.

✉ **Oystermouth Road, Swansea**
☎ **01792 649126**

Techniquest

Science and engineering are explained by hands-on equipment.

✉ **Stuart Street, Cardiff Bay**
☎ **029 20475475**

Welsh Wildlife Centre

A pleasant zoo surrounded by beautiful countryside. Otters are a particular speciality.

✉ **Cilgerran near Cardigan**
☎ **01239 621600**

Theatres, Art & Culture

North Wales

Theatre Gwynedd
Modern theatre with performances in English and Welsh. The summer programme is more geared to tourists.

✉ **Deiniol Road, Bangor**
☎ **01248 35708**

North Wales Theatre
The most important theatre in north Wales in a modern building with 1,500 seats. Varied programme with top productions from Cardiff and London.

✉ **The Promenade, Llandudno**
☎ **01492 872000**

European Centre for Traditional and Regional Cultures
Music and dance performances by groups representing ethnic and cultural minorities.

✉ **Castle Street, Llangollen**
☎ **01978 861514**

Theatre Clwyd
Modern theatre that not only serves the region but also works to preserve and promote Welsh culture.

✉ **Mold**
☎ **01352 755114**

Central Wales

Aberystwyth Arts Centre
The centre is a guarantee of quality.

✉ **University campus Penglais Hill**
☎ **01970 623232**

Theatre Brycheiniog
Stylish new venue on the quayside for theatre, music and dance, with 436 seats.

✉ **Canal Wharf, Brecon**
☎ **01874 611622/622838**

Wyeside Arts Centre
One of the few theatres in the Welsh borders, mainly serving a regional role. Varied programme in the renovated 19th-century Assembly Rooms.

✉ **Builth Wells** ☎ **01982 552555**

Theatre Mwldan
Provincial theatre with mainly local and regional productions of various kinds.

✉ **Bath House Road, Cardigan**
☎ **01239 621200**

Albert Hall
A venue geared to classical and traditional performance art.

✉ **Ithon Road, Llandrindod Wells** ☎ **01597 825677**

Pavilion
Various productions, including shows and concerts.

✉ **Spa Road, Llandrindod Wells** ☎ **01597 823421**

Tabernacl
Cultural centre in an old chapel, with a museum of modern art and a programme of performance art.

✉ **Y Tabernacl, Machynlleth**
☎ **01654 703355**

Theatre Hafren
Theatre of modest proportions with varying programme of drama, dance and music.

✉ **Llanidloes Road, Newtown**
☎ **01686 625007**

South Wales

Lyric Theatre
Small theatre with a mainly regional role.

✉ **Carmarthen**
☎ **01267 232632**

Choir Singing
'From the moment they stop crying, babies start singing', wrote Giraldus Cambrensis in about 1191. Indeed the Welsh love singing. There are numerous choirs, especially in the industrialised regions, where they have made a significant contribution to a sense of community. If you are unable to go to a performance, you could always go to a public rehearsal. The local tourist office can advise you on reservations.

Penillion
This very special, traditional form of singing can be heard at an eisteddfod. The harp accompaniment plays a well-known melody (hymn, national anthem), after which the singer comes in in a different key. The intention is to weave the two together to create a beautiful effect. Both musicians must finish at the same time. This is as difficult as it sounds.

Seaside Theatres
Many seaside resorts have theatres offering a summer programme geared to tourists. These can be found in Colwyn Bay (Colwyn Theatre), Rhyl (Pavilion Theatre), Porthcawl (Grand Pavilion), and Tenby (the Valance Pavilion).

Open-air Performances
Many well-known castles and gardens stage open-air performances in the summer months, especially music and theatre. Enquire at the local tourist offices. A well-known location is Oystermouth Castle near Swansea.

Torch Theatre
Theatre of modest size with a varied and professional programme.
✉ Milford Haven
☎ 01646 695267

Cardiff
Cardiff International Arena
This is *the* place for big concerts, especially pop singers and pop groups, but also by famous classical stars such as Pavarotti and Kiri Te Kanawa.
✉ Mary Ann Street, Cardiff
☎ 029 20224488

Chapter Arts Centre
A programme which is as extensive as it is varied. Many forms of performance art, including theatre and dance. New talents are given a chance. Also some of the more offbeat films are shown here.
✉ Market Road, Canton
☎ 029 20399666

New Theatre
Theatre opened in 1906 for mainly classical stage productions, West End shows and ballet. Also home of the Welsh National Opera until the Millennium Centre on Cardiff Bay is opened.
✉ Park Place, Cardiff
☎ 029 20878889

St David's Hall
The most important concert hall in Wales. Home of the BBC National Orchestra of Wales. Also host to the Cardiff Singer of Wales Competition, the Welsh Proms, the St David's Hall Orchestral Concert Series, as well as some pop and rock concerts.

✉ The Hayes, Cardiff
☎ 029 20878444

Sherman Theatre
Emphasis on modern, contemporary and sometimes experimental theatre.
✉ Senghenydd Road, Cardiff
☎ 029 20230451

Swansea
Brangwyn Hall, The Guildhall
This fine hall is a prominent part of the town hall and is used especially for (classical) concerts. It is also the headquarters of the annual Swansea Festival (October).
✉ Outside the centre, via Oystermouth Road
☎ 01792 635489

Dylan Thomas Theatre
Intimate theatre near the marina.
✉ Gloucester Place
☎ 01792 473238

Grand Theatre
A fine theatre – one of the best regional theatres in the country.
✉ Singleton Street
☎ 01792 475715

Taliesin Arts Centre
This centre is part of the university and stages theatre, dance, music and film productions.
✉ University of Wales, Swansea
☎ 01792 296883

Ty Lien
Part of the National Literature Centre and as such a legacy from the Year of Literature (1995).
✉ Somerset Place
☎ 01792 463892

Long-distance Walking

Walking or hiking is as popular in Wales as it is elsewhere in Britain. Many people use their days off for a hike of one or more days. Routes varying in length have been set out for this purpose. Most are well signposted and it is often possible to buy separate brochures, or even booklets on these routes. Naturally, it is not necessary to walk the full length of a path. You can restrict yourself to the section of your choice. Below is a selection.

Long-distance Footpaths

Offa's Dyke Path

Follows the border between England and Wales, partly along the 8th-century Offa's Dyke itself, from Chepstow in the south to Prestatyn in the north. Length: 288km (179 miles).

Cambrian Way

For energetic walkers who wish to go straight through the interior of Wales, across the hills and mountain ridges, from the south (Cardiff) to the north (Conwy), or vice versa. Length: 440km (274 miles). This route is only described, not signposted.

North Wales Path

A varied hike with beautiful views, which leads from Prestatyn to Bangor, always within a short distance to the coast. Length: 78km (48 miles).

Glyndwr's Way

A route that gives the walker ample opportunity to explore central Wales. Named after the 15th-century Welsh rebel who long maintained his rebellion against the English in this area. Starting points: Welshpool, Knighton and Machynlleth. Length: 212km (132 miles).

Dyfi Valley Walk

From Aberdovey to the southern point of Bala Lake, and then through the Dovey (Dyfi) Valley to Borth on Cardigan Bay. Length: 172km (107 miles).

Severn Valley Way

Only the first part of this 440km (273-mile) trip, namely from Aberystwyth to Montgomery/Welshpool goes through Wales. After that it leads through Shrewsbury, Worcester and Gloucester to Bristol.

Pembrokeshire Coast Path

Along the coast of the national park of the same name, from St Dogmaels near Cardigan to Amroth beyond Tenby. Length: 299km (186 miles).

Wye Valley Walk

Between Chepstow and Rhayader, through the wooded Wye Valley and then across the hills of Herefordshire (England) and Powys (Wales). Length: 230km (143 miles).

Usk Valley Walk

From Brecon through the Brecon Beacons to the estuary of the Usk at Newport, Gwent. Length: 80km (50 miles).

Short Walking Routes

Walking in Nature Reserves

You can walk in the woods and dunes of Newborough Warren on Anglesey, the dunes of Ynyslas and the bird reserve Ynys Hir, both near the estuary of the Dovey (Borth), Kenfig Pool near Porthcawl, Oxwich in Gower, as well as the nature areas mentioned in this guide, such as South Stack (Holy Island), Lake Vyrnwy, Cwm Idwal, the islands of Skomer and Skokholm, and Worms Head.

Aberglaslyn Pass

Along the Glaslyn, across a section of the former Welsh Highland Railway. Length: 6km (4 miles).

Clywedog Walk

In the vicinity of Wrexham. Length: 13.4km (8½ miles).

Mawddach Trail

Trail runs from Barmouth to Dolgellau along the shores of the Mawddach. Length: 15km (9½ miles).

Gwaun Valley Walks

Three walks that have been set out by the national park authorities through a dense, remote valley. Sections of approximately 4km (2½ miles) can be combined with longer routes.

Carreg Cennen Walk

In the vicinity of the castle of the same name, on the western edge of the Brecon Beacons National Park.

Three Castles Walk

Links the triangle of Grosmont, Skenfrith and White castles. Total length: 29km (18 miles).

Good Walking Areas

Clocaenog Forest

Woods with artificial lakes. Information: Bod Petrual Visitor Centre, south of the B5105, 12km (7½ miles) from Ruthin.

Gwydyr Forest

Extensive forests of the Forestry Commission, north of Betws-y-coed. Information and route descriptions: Y Stablau Visitor Centre, Betws-y-coed.

Coed y Brenin Forest

Information on the many opportunities for walking and cycling are available from the Maesgwm Forest Visitor Centre on the A470, north of Dolgellau.

Rheidol Forest

Together with the Ystwyth and the Hafren forests, the Rheidol Forest make a refreshing change from the undulating moorland of central Wales. Blwch Nant yr Arian Visitor Centre on the A44, east of Aberystwyth.

Llyn Brianne and Brecon Beacons Forests

The Tywi, Irfon and Crychan forests stretch out north and east of the lonely Llyn Britanne. In the Brecon Beacons, the Coed Taf, Talybont and Mynydd-Du forests are of interest. Information: Garwnant Visitor Centre on the A470, 8km (5 miles) north of Merthyr Tydfil.

The Valleys

In the western valleys: Crynant, Rheola and Margam forests. The Afan Argoed Country Park (via the A4107) has an information centre. There are also bicycles for hire. In the eastern valleys: Ebbw, Rhondda and St Gwynno forests. And near the border with England, the woods of Tintern and Wentwood. Information from the tourist office next to Tintern Abbey.

Active Holidays

Mountaineering
The national parks of Snowdonia and the Brecon Beacons provide good opportunities for mountaineering. Details from the information centres in the parks themselves or from the Plas y Brenin National Mountain Centre in Capel Curig (near Betws-y-coed) or the Brecon Beacons Mountain Centre in Libanus (near Brecon).

Cycling
Cycling Wales is a Welsh Tourist Board brochure that lists organisations providing cycling trips, describes routes, and lists rental addresses. The National Cycle Route from Cardiff or Chepstow to Anglesey is 384km (239 miles) long – of course, you can choose to complete only parts of the route. Shorter sections may include the Taff Trail from Cardiff to Brecon (83km/52 miles) and to the routes from Hay-on-Wye via Builth Wells to Machynlleth, and via Dolgellau to Barmouth. A recently finished route, named the Celtic Trail, links Kidwelly via Swansea with Newport, Gwent. Particularly good cycling or mountain-biking areas include the Elan Valley, the Gower peninsula, the Coed Brenin and the Brechfa Forest, and in the north the Lleyn peninsula and Anglesey .

Golf
You need never look far for a golf course in Wales, as there are nearly 180 of them. They are all listed in a Welsh Tourist Board brochure.

Horse riding
There are opportunities for horse riding throughout Wales. This usually means hikes of half a day, one day or longer. The Welsh Tourist Board brochure *Discovering Wales on Horseback* is useful. Popular areas include the surroundings of Conwy, southern Anglesey, Dolgellau, various parts of Pembrokeshire, the Gower peninsula, Rhayader and surroundings, and the Brecon Beacons, in particular around the Vale of Ewyas, Brecon and Crickhowell.

Paragliding
Paragliding is becoming increasingly popular – there are opportunities in Llanberis, Builth Wells and Abergavenny.

Water sports
The Wye (Glasbury) and Tryweryn (near Bala) are suitable for white-water canoeing. The Usk, Conwy and Llygwy also offer opportunities if the water-level is sufficiently high. The Dee and Teifi are calmer, as are the estuaries of the Daugleddau (Milford Haven), Conwy and Towy rivers. The southwestern coasts of Gower and Pembrokeshire are best for surfing. Windsurfing is possible on Lake Bala, Oxwich Bay (Gower) and Dale Roads (Pembrokeshire). Rougher conditions apply in Lllangennith (Gower) and Hell's Mouth (Lleyn). Sailing is popular in the harbours of Neyland, Swansea, Aberystwyth and Pwllheli. Also in the more sheltered Menai Strait and the Daugleddau.

Be Active
The annually Wales Tourist Board brochure *Activity Wales* contains invaluable information on opportunities for active holidays. It also lists addresses of centres and organisations that offer courses. In addition, the WTB publishes brochures on walking, horse riding, cycling and mountain biking, angling, water sports and golfing.

Bog Snorkelling – a Curious Sport
Every year in August, Llanwrtyd Wells (central Wales) holds the World Bog Snorkelling Championships. Participants attempt to complete the 100m route through a muddy, pungent peat bog as fast as possible whilst snorkelling. They are allowed to come up for air twice and check that they are heading in the right direction. The curious sight of these 'swimmers' ploughing through mud draws spectators and participants from afar.

What's On When

Festivals of Wales
There are more than 60 festivals of varying size in Wales every year. For the latest information, contact:
Festivals of Wales
PO Box 20, Conwy LL32 8ZO
☎ 01492 573760.

Brecon Jazz Festival
This festival is held every year in August and is widely regarded as the best and most exciting in Wales. Some of the world's best jazz musicians come here, both groups and individual artists. They perform not only in pubs and public buildings, such as the museum, the town hall and the guildhall, but also in the streets. For further information, contact:
The Brecon Jazz Festival Ltd
The Watton, Brecon LD3 7EF
☎ 01874 610273.

February
• Six Nations Rugby Championship, Millennium Stadium, Cardiff (runs through to April)

March
• St David's Day (1 March, festivities in various places around the country)

May
• Hay-on-Wye Literature Festival
• Victorian Extravaganza, Llandudno
• Swansea Show
• St David's Cathedral Festival of classical music (sometimes also early June)

June
• Beaumaris Festival, Anglesey
• Criccieth Festival of Music and the Arts (sometimes July)
• National Eisteddfod for young people, alternately in north and south Wales
• Cardiff Singer of the World Competition (odd-numbered years: 2001, 2003, etc.)
• Man versus Horse Marathon, Llanwrtyd Wells
• Three Peaks Yacht Race, Barmouth to Fort William
• Drovers Walk, Llanwrtyd Wells
• Gregynog Festival for classical music, Gregynog Hall near Newtown

July
• International Music Eisteddfod, Llangollen
• Royal Welsh Show, Builth Wells – *the* agricultural show for Wales
• Welsh Proms, Cardiff
• Gower Festival
• Fishguard International Music Festival

• Cardiff Festival (runs until August)
• Conwy Festival
• Conwy River Festival

August
• Llanwrtyd Wells Festival
• United County Show, Carmarthen
• Anglesey County Show, Llangefni
• Royal National Eisteddfod, alternately in north and south Wales
• Brecon Jazz Festival
• Llandrindod Wells Victorian Festival
• Machynlleth Festival

September
• Tenby Arts Festival
• Celtic Festival, Machynlleth
• Usk Show
• Vale of Glamorgan Festival
• Swansea Cockle Festival

October
• Swansea Festival of Music and the Arts
• Llandudno October Festival for music, poetry and art

November
• Welsh International Film Festival, Cardiff
• Mid-Wales Beer Festival, Llanwrtyd Wells

Practical Matters

Above: *the manual air
gondola in Aberaeron*

TIME DIFFERENCES

| GMT
12 noon | British Summer
1PM | Germany →
1–2PM | USA (NY) ←
7AM | Ottawa ←
7AM | Spain →
1PM |

BEFORE YOU GO

WHAT YOU NEED

		UK	USA	Germany	Netherlands	Spain
● Required ○ Suggested ▲ Not required	Some countries require a passport to remain valid for a minimum period (usually at least six months) beyond the date of entry – contact their consulate or embassy or your travel agent for details.					
Passport		▲	●	●	●	●
Visa (Regulations can vary – check before you travel)		▲	▲	▲	▲	▲
Onward or Return Ticket		▲	○	○	○	○
Health Inoculations		▲	▲	▲	▲	▲
Health Documentation		▲	●	●	●	●
Travel Insurance		○	○	○	○	○
Driving Licence (national)		●	●	●	●	●
Car Insurance Certificate (if own car)		▲	●	●	●	●
Car Registration Document (if own car)		▲	●	●	●	●

WHEN TO GO

Wales

High season

Low season

6°C	7°C	10°C	13°C	15°C	18°C	20°C	20°C	17°C	12°C	9°C	7°C
JAN	FEB	MAR	APR	MAY	JUN	JUL	AUG	SEP	OCT	NOV	DEC

Very wet   Wet   Sun   Sun/Showers

TOURIST OFFICES

In Wales
Wales Tourist Board
Brunel House
2 Fitzalan Road
Cardiff CF2 0UY
☎ 029 20499909
Fax 029 20485031
www.visitwales.com

In England
Wales Tourist Board
1 Regent Street
W1R 1XT
☎ 020 78083838

In USA
British Tourist Authority
551 5th Avenue Suite 701
New York 10176
☎ 877-8997199

118

WHEN YOU ARE THERE

ARRIVING

Wales has one international airport: Cardiff. There are direct flights from most major UK airports and some other European cities. The airport is 19km (12 miles) west of the city centre. There is a fast bus service: the X91 (in the evening the 345) and the X5 go every hour. From London, it is possible take a coach from Victoria Coach Station or Heathrow Airport to the principality. National Express 201 travels from Heathrow to Cardiff and Swansea. For central and north Wales, you will first need to go to Victoria Coach Station to take the 420 or 545, respectively. Visitors wishing to travel by train should go via Paddington (south Wales) or Euston (central and north Wales).

Manchester Airport (National Express 390 for the north and 325 for central Wales from Manchester Coach Station) and Birmingham Airport (National Express 420 for central Wales and 545 for north Wales) can also be used as approach routes. In such cases, there are also good railway links with central Wales (via Shrewsbury) and north Wales (via Chester).

MONEY

Britain's currency is the pound sterling (£), issued in notes of £5, £10, £20, £50. There are 100 pence (p) to one pound and coins come in denominations of 1p, 2p, 5p, 10p, 50p, £1 and £2. Traveller's cheques may be accepted by some hotels, shops and restaurants. Sterling traveller's cheques are the most convenient.

TIME

Wales, like the rest of the UK, is on Greenwich Mean Time (GMT) in winter, but from late March until late October British Summer Times (BST, i.e. GMT + 1) operates.

CUSTOMS

YES
From another EU country for your personal use (guidelines):
800 cigarettes, 200 cigars, 1 kilogram of tobacco
10 litres of spirits (over 22%)
20 litres of aperitifs
90 litres of wine, of which 60 litres can be sparkling wine
110 litres of beer

From a non-EU country for your personal use
200 cigarettes OR 50 cigars OR 250 grams of tobacco
1 litre of spirits (over 22%)
2 litres of fortified wine (e.g. sherry), sparkling wine or other liqueurs
2 litres still wine
50 ml of perfume
250 ml of eau de toilette

Travellers under 17 years of age are not entitled to the tobacco and alcohol allowances.

No
Unlicensed drugs, firearms, ammunition, offensive weapons, obscene material, unlicensed animals, counterfeit and copied goods, meat and poultry

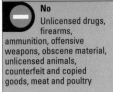

119

CONSULATES

Canada
020 72586600

USA
029 20786633

WHEN YOU ARE THERE

TOURIST OFFICES

- Wales Tourist Board
  Brunel House, 2 Fitzalan Road,
  Cardiff CF2 0UY
  ☎ 029 20499909, e-mail
  info@tourism.wales.gov.uk
- North Wales Tourism
  77 Conway Road, Colwyn
  Bay LL29 7LN
  ☎ 01492 531731
  e-mail croeso@nwt.co.uk
  www.nwt.co.uk
- Mid Wales Tourism
  The Station, Machynlleth,
  Powys SY20 8TG
  ☎ 01654 703526
  e-mail mwt@mid-wales-tourism.org.uk
  www.mid-wales-tourism.org.uk
- Tourism South & West
  Wales
  Charter Court, Enterprise
  Park, Swansea SA7 9DB
  ☎ 01792 781212, e-mail
  marketing@tsww.com
- Cardiff Visitor Centre
  16 Wood Street, Cardiff
  CF10 1EF
  ☎ 029 20227281
  e-mail NicolaM@cardiff-marketing.co.uk
  www.cardiffmarketing.co.uk

National Parks

- Brecon Beacons
  7 Glamorgan Street,
  Brecon LD3 7DP
  ☎ 01874 624437
- Pembrokeshire Coast
  Winch Lane,
  Haverfordwest SA61 1PY
  ☎ 01437 764636
- Snowdonia
  Penrhyndeudraeth
  LL48 6LF
  ☎ 01766 770274

NATIONAL HOLIDAYS

J	F	M	A	M	J	J	A	S	O	N	D
1		(1)	(1)	2			1				2

1 Jan	New Year's Day
Mar/Apr	Good Friday, Easter Monday
First Mon in May	May Day Bank Holiday
Last Mon in May	Late May Bank Holiday
Last Mon in Aug	August Bank Holiday
25 Dec	Christmas Day
26 Dec	Boxing Day

Almost all attractions close on Christmas Day. On other holidays some attractions may open with reduced hours. There are no general rules regarding the opening times of restaurants and shops, so check before making a special journey.

OPENING HOURS

○ Shops	● Attractions/museums
● Offices	● Post ofcies
● Banks	● Pharmacies

The times shown above are traditional opening hours. Many shops throughout Wales, especially those in the cities and large towns (but increasingly elsewhere), open for longer, and many of them now open on Sundays too. High-street banks are sometimes open Saturday mornings and bureaux de change are open daily until late. Many of the museums and visitor attractions detailed in this guide may close for one day a week, and often on special occasions. It is always wise to check the times by telephoning first. When pharmacies are closed you'll find a sign in the window giving details of the nearest one that is on 24-hour duty. In the countryside, shops close one afternoon a week, and often also for lunch from 1–2.

DRIVE ON THE
LEFT

TOILETS
FREE

PUBLIC TRANSPORT

The Welsh Tourist Board issues a useful public-transport brochure with all train, bus and boat routes. The national information number is ☎ 0891 910910. **Discount passes** There are various opportunities to travel at reduced rates. The Freedom of Wales Flexi-Pass allows unlimited train travel for eight within fifteen days or four within eight days; the card is also valid on buses during the full fifteen or eight days. You can also buy a regional seven-day North & Mid Wales Flexi-Rover or a Freedom of South Wales Flexi-Rover, or day cards such as a Cambrian Coaster Day Ranger, a Mid Wales Day Ranger or a Cardiff Valley Lines Day Ranger. Bus companies also have their own day-rider or rover tickets for one day (sometimes also for more than one day).

For rail discount cards valid throughout the United Kingdom, contact the Rail Europe Travel Centre, 179 Piccadilly, London W15 9BA ☎ 08705 848848, www.britrail.com. For current rail timetables contact Railtrack ☎ 08457 484950.

 Trains The possibilities of exploring Wales by train are limited. There is a reasonably dense railway network in the south, especially in the Valleys and along the coast. Two lines run through beautiful countryside to serve central Wales from Shrewsbury, and in the north there is a coastal route and a beautiful section straight through Snowdonia. Enquiries ☎ 0345 484950. It is also possible to make use of the nine Great Little Trains lines, which are mostly for sightseeing: ☎ 01983 810441.

 Coaches From London, Bristol, Birmingham, Manchester and other large English cities. National Express coaches travel to the most important places in Wales ☎ 0990 808080. There is also a north–south route straight through Wales ☎ 01970 617951.

 Regional buses In the more populous areas, the bus is a convenient form of transport. In isolated regions, in particular in central Wales, not all villages and hamlets are served by buses, or the frequency is low. Consult the public transport brochure before departure.

Car rental Avis (☎ 01446 719569), Europcar (☎ 01446 711924) and Hertz (☎ 01446 711722) have branches at Cardiff Airport. It is advisable to reserve in peak season.

DRIVING

 Speed limit on motorways and dual carriageways: **112kph (70mph)**

 Speed limit on main roads: 80–100kph **(50–60mph)**

 Speed limit on minor roads: **50–65kph (30–40mph)**

 Must be worn in front seats at all times and in rear seats where fitted.

 A roads (green signs) are main roads. B roads (white signs) are local roads, while M roads (blue signs) indicate motorways. Road signs are bilingual, in Welsh and English.

 Unleaded petrol is available everywhere in Wales. The number of outlets for LPG, however, is limited. In isolated areas, pumps may be very far apart. Some are closed on Sunday. The price level – compared with North America and the Continent – can be on the high side.

 SOS telephones are found mainly along motorways, also sometimes in isolated regions. If you break down driving your own car and are a member of an AA-affiliated motoring club, you can call the AA ☎ 0800 887766. If your car is hired, follow the instructions in the documentation.

121

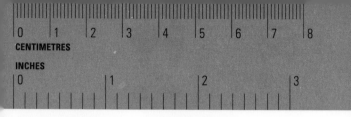

CENTIMETRES

INCHES

PERSONAL SAFETY

The cities, towns and villages of the Wales are generally safe places to visit; in the larger cities in the south you need to watch out for car theft, handbag snatchers and pickpockets. You can help minimise the risk of personal crime:

- Don't leave valuable items in the car
- Beware of pickpockets in markets and other busy places
- Don't carry too much money. Leave valuables and passports in your hotel safe.

Police assistance:
☎ **999**
from any call box

TELEPHONES

Public telephones on the street and in bars, hotels and restaurants accept 10p, 20p, 50p, £1 and £2 coins, others can be used only with a phone card (available at kiosks and post offices). The charges are significantly lower than when calling from a hotel room.

International dialling codes from the UK to:

Canada:	00 1
USA:	00 1

POST

Every town and most large villages have at least one post office. They are open Mon–Fri 9–5:30, Sat 9–1. Smaller post offices close at lunchtime from 1–2. Stamps are also available at some kiosks, newsagents and shops selling postcards.

ELECTRICITY

The power supply in Britain is 240 volts. Sockets only accept three-square-pin

plugs, so an adaptor is needed for Continental and American appliances. A transformer is needed for appliances operating on 110–120 volts.

TIPS/GRATUITIES

Yes ✓ No ✗		
Restaurant (service not included)	✓	10–12%
Tour Guides	✓	£1–2
Taxis	✓	10%
Porters	✓	£1/bag
		or case
Chambermaids	✓	£2
Hairdressers	✓	£1–2
Cloakroom attendants	✓	£1
Toilet	✗	
Theatre/cinema ushers	✗	

What to photograph: impressive castles, narrow-gauge railways with steam engines, green valleys, rugged mountainscapes, cliff coastlines with bays, ravines, sandy beaches and rock formations.
Restrictions: where photography is not allowed, this will be clearly indicated on warning signs.
Buying photographic film: all kinds of films of well-known makes as well as batteries are for sale and reasonably priced. Slides are expensive.

HEALTH

Insurance
Nationals of EU and certain other countries can get free medical treatment in Britain with the relevant documentation, although private medical insurance is still advised, and is essential for all other visitors. See Form 111 obtainable from a post office. Prescriptions need to be paid for, but you may be able to claim this back on insurance.

Dental Services
Dental treatment is very limited under the National Health Service scheme and even nationals of the EU usually have to pay. However, private medical insurance should cover the costs.

Weather
As the climate in Wales can be unreliable, waterproof clothing and an umbrella are essential. On some days it may also be cold, especially in spring and autumn, so it is advisable to take a warm jumper. Visitors who wish to walk, for example along the coast paths, should take sturdy, waterproof footwear.

Drugs/medicines
Prescription and non-prescription drugs and medicines are available from pharmacies. Medicines that do not require a prescription are often available from supermarkets and pharmacies.

Safe Water
Tap water is safe to drink. Mineral water is fairly expensive, especially in restaurants. There are some good Welsh brands of mineral water.

CONCESSIONS

Students/children and senior citizens There are various situations in which children, students and senior citizens may be able to obtain concessions. This applies to public transport, as well as to museums and tourist attractions. You will need to show identification, however, for example a Student Identity Card or similar pass.
If you intend to visit many **CADW** (Welsh Historic Monuments) sights, it may be worthwhile to become a member or to purchase a 3- or 7-day explorer ticket. This saves a considerable amount of money.

CLOTHING SIZES

UK	USA	Europe	
36	36	46	
38	38	48	
40	40	50	
42	42	52	Suits
44	44	54	
46	46	56	
7	8	41	
7.5	8.5	42	
8.5	9.5	43	Shoes
9.5	10.5	44	
10.5	11.5	45	
11	12	46	
14.5	14.5	37	
15	15	38	
15.5	15.5	39/40	Shirts
16	16	41	
16.5	16.5	42	
17	17	43	
8	6	34	
10	8	36	
12	10	38	Dresses
14	12	40	
16	14	42	
18	16	44	
4.5	6	38	
5	6.5	38	
5.5	7	39	Shoes
6	7.5	39	
6.5	8	40	
7	8.5	41	

WHEN DEPARTING

- If travelling by coach, rail or ferry you must reserve well in advance, particularly in the peak season and national holidays.
- If travelling by air you should confirm your return flight at least 48 hours before departure.
- Avoid the motorway around London (M25) during the morning rush hour. It is also advisable not to travel far on the Friday and Monday of a bank-holiday weekend.

LANGUAGE

Wales has been officially bilingual since 1967. Nearly all inhabitants speak English; Welsh is spoken only by 20 per cent of the population, especially in the more remote countryside of northwest, west and southwest Wales. Celtic Welsh, one of the oldest living languages of Europe, belongs to the Celtic branch of the Indo-European languages, but it has too little in common with English for many words to be recognisable. Pronunciation presents a few problems, especially the use of many consonants in rapid succession (such as *bwlch*) and some sounds that are pronounced in an unpredictable way (*ll* is pronounced as a guttural *gl*). Until recently there was a steady decline in the number of speakers, but a renewed interest in Welsh culture and Welsh-language programmes on television has led to the numbers stabilising. Welsh is also part of the national curriculum for schools in Wales and now all children learn a standardized version.

Everyday Welsh

good morning	*bore da*	Welsh	*Cymreag*
good day	*dydd da*	Welshman	*Cymro*
good evening	*noswaith dda*	Wales	*Cymru*
good night	*nos da*	good	*da*
thanks	*diolch*	sheep	*dafad, dafaid*
thank you very much	*diolch yn fawr iawn*	health	*lechyd da!*
		best wishes	*dymuniadau gorau*
welcome	*croeso*	how are you?	*sut mae?*

Place-name derivations

estuary	*aber*	road	*heol*
river	*afon*	slate	*llech*
small	*bach/fach*	church, parish	*llan*
top, peak	*ban/fan*	lake, water pool	*llyn*
grave	*bedd*	stone	*maen*
house of worship	*betws*	open field	*maes*
		large	*mawr, fawr*
source of river, start of valley	*blaen*	church, churchyard	*merthyr*
pass, ravine	*bwlch*	treeless hill	*moel, foel*
fort	*caer, gear*	marsh, mudflat	*morfa*
stone, rock	*carreg*	mountain	*mynydd*
wood, forest	*coed, coedwig*	stream	*nant*
red	*coch, goch*	cave	*ogof*
valley	*cwm*	top, end	*pen*
junction	*cymer*	village	*pentre*
David	*Dewi*	mansion	*plas*
fort, city	*dinas*	bridge	*pont*
black	*du, ddu*	puddle, pool	*pwll*
church	*eglwys*	slope	*rhiw*
border	*ffin*	heather	*rhos*
river, verge, shore	*glan*	settlement, town house	*tre* *tŷ*
valley	*glyn*	high, higher, highest	*uchaf*
common, meadow	*gwaun*	island	*ynys*
old	*hen*	bend	*ystwyth*

Index

Acknowledgements
AA Publishing and Kosmos-Z&K wish to thank the following photographers and libraries for their assistance in the preparation of this book:

AUTOMOBILE ASSOCIATION PHOTOLIBRARY 30, 35, 37, 46, 47, 56, 71, 74, 81, 82, 83, 84, 85, 86, 88, 89a, 89b, 90, 117a, 122b, BRITISH TOURIST BOARD 117b, CADW: WELSH HISTORIC MONUMENTS CROWN COPYRIGHT 5a, 17, 24, 77, DAVID LINDSEY 12, 13, 14, 42, 50, 51, 54a, 54b, 55a, 55b, 66, 122c, DYFFRYN GARDENS 76, EISTEDDFOD LLANGOLLEN 91b, GUUS BERKIEN 1, 2, 5hb, 8, 9, 15a, 16, 18, 19, 21, 22, 23, 25, 26, 27b, 31, 32, 33, 34, 40, 41, 44, 45, 48, 49, 52, 53, 60, 61, 62, 64, 65, 67, 68, 69, 70, 72, 75, 78, 79,80, 87, 91a, 122a, HUW EVANS PICTURE AGENCY CARDIFF 8, JEREMY MOORE 36, NORTH WALES TOURISM 11, THE NATIONAL BOTANIC GARDEN OF WALES 20, THE NATIONAL LIBRARY OF WALES 10, TOURISM AND LEISURE DEPARTMENT, CONWY COUNTY BOROUGH COUNCIL 27a, 39, TOURISM SECTION LLANDINDROD WELLS 57, WALES TOURIST BOARD PHOTO LIBRARY 6, 7, 15b, 43

Dear Essential Traveller

Your comments, opinions and recommendations are very important to us. So please help us to improve our travel guides by taking a few minutes to complete this simple questionnaire.

You do not need a stamp (unless posted outside the UK). If you do not want to cut this page from your guide, then photocopy it or write your answers on a plain sheet of paper.

Send to: **The Editor, AA World Travel Guides, FREEPOST SCE 4598, Basingstoke RG21 4GY.**

Your recommendations...

We always encourage readers' recommendations for restaurants, nightlife or shopping – if your recommendation is used in the next edition of the guide, we will send you a *FREE* AA *Essential* **Guide** of your choice. Please state below the establishment name, location and your reasons for recommending it.

_____
_____
_____
_____

Please send me **AA *Essential*** _____
(*see list of titles inside the front cover*)

About this guide...

Which title did you buy?
   AA *Essential* _____
Where did you buy it? _____
When? m m / y y

Why did you choose an AA *Essential* Guide? _____
_____
_____
_____
_____

Did this guide meet your expectations?
   Exceeded ☐   Met all ☐   Met most ☐   Fell below ☐
   Please give your reasons _____
_____
_____
_____

continued on next page...

Were there any aspects of this guide that you particularly liked? _____

_____

_____

_____

Is there anything we could have done better? _____

_____

_____

_____

_____

About you...

Name (*Mr/Mrs/Ms*) _____

Address _____

_____

_____ Postcode _____

Daytime tel nos _____

Which age group are you in?

Under 25 ☐   25–34 ☐   35–44 ☐   45–54 ☐   55–64 ☐   65+ ☐

How many trips do you make a year?

Less than one ☐   One ☐   Two ☐   Three or more ☐

Are you an AA member? Yes ☐   No ☐

About your trip...

When did you book? m m / y y   When did you travel? m m / y y

How long did you stay? _____

Was it for business or leisure? _____

Did you buy any other travel guides for your trip?

If yes, which ones? _____

_____

Thank you for taking the time to complete this questionnaire. Please send
it to us as soon as possible, and remember, you do not need a stamp
(*unless posted outside the UK*).

Happy Holidays!